George IV

Pocket BIOGRAPHIES

Series Editor C.S. Nicholls

Highly readable brief lives of those who have played a significant part in history, and whose contributions still influence contemporary culture.

Pocket BIOGRAPHIES

George IV

MICHAEL DE-LA-NOY

SUTTON PUBLISHING

First published in the United Kingdom in 1998 by
Sutton Publishing Limited · Phoenix Mill
Thrupp · Stroud · Gloucestershire · GL5 2BU

British Library Cataloguing in Publication Data
A catalogue record for this book is available from the British
Library

ISBN 0 7509 1821 7

Typeset in 13/18pt Perpetua.
Typesetting and origination by
Sutton Publishing Limited.
Printed in Great Britain by
The Guernsey Press Company Limited,
Guernsey, Channel Islands.

For Peter Parker
fellow biographer and friend

Also by Michael De-la-Noy

Elgar: The Man
Denton Welch: The Making of a Writer
The Honours System
Acting as Friends: The Story of the Samaritans
Eddy: The Life of Edward Sackville-West
Michael Ramsey: A Portrait
Windsor Castle: Past and Present
Exploring Oxford
The Church of England: A Portrait
The Queen Behind the Throne
The King Who Never Was: The Story of Frederick, Prince of Wales
Mervyn Stockwood: A Lonely Life
Scott of the Antarctic

EDITED BY MICHAEL DE-LA-NOY

The Journals of Denton Welch
The Collected Short Writings of Denton Welch

CONTENTS

AUTHOR'S NOTE

No one who attempts a biography of George IV need apologise for relying heavily on previous research undertaken by Christopher Hibbert, one of the most accomplished and productive historians writing today. There really is only one major life of George IV, and that is Hibbert's, in two volumes, dealing initially with his years as Prince of Wales and secondly as Regent and King. For anybody wishing to learn more about this monarch, Christopher Hibbert will supply an erudite yet immensely readable romp through Georgian England.

Over many years Christopher Hibbert's biographies and social histories have provided information and pleasure to thousands of readers, not least to myself, and it is a privilege to have this opportunity of acknowledging his prodigious industry and enviable gifts.

Michael De-la-Noy

Hove, 1998

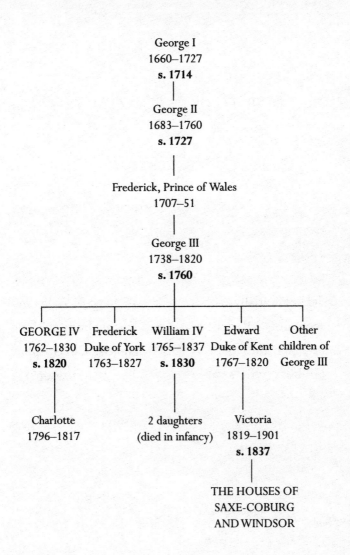

George I
1660–1727
s. 1714

George II
1683–1760
s. 1727

Frederick, Prince of Wales
1707–51

George III
1738–1820
s. 1760

GEORGE IV	Frederick	William IV	Edward	Other
1762–1830	Duke of York	1765–1837	Duke of Kent	children of
s. 1820	1763–1827	**s. 1830**	1767–1820	George III

Charlotte
1796–1817

2 daughters
(died in infancy)

Victoria
1819–1901
s. 1837

THE HOUSES OF
SAXE-COBURG
AND WINDSOR

Abbreviated family tree of George IV
(**s.** = date of succession)

CHRONOLOGY

12 Aug. 1762	Born at St James's Palace
	Created Prince of Wales
1783	Given Carlton House
	Takes seat in House of Lords
	First visit to Brighton
1784	Canvasses for Fox
1785	Marries Maria Fitzherbert
1787	Henry Holland starts work on Brighton Pavilion
	Becomes Freemason
1788	Onset of George III's insanity
1792	Makes maiden speech in House of Lords
1794	Countess of Jersey becomes mistress
1795	Marries Caroline of Brunswick
1796	Birth of daughter, Charlotte
1806	Commission of Enquiry into conduct of wife
	Marchioness of Hertford becomes mistress
1810	Receives honorary Oxford doctorate
1811	Appointed Regent
1815	John Nash transforms Brighton Pavilion
1816	Daughter marries Prince Leopold of Saxe-Coburg-Saalfeld
1817	Death of daughter

1818	Death of mother, Queen Charlotte
1819	Birth of niece, later Queen Victoria
1820	Succeeds to the throne
	The Queen on trial
	Marchioness of Conyngham becomes mistress
	Rebuilds Buckingham House
1821	Coronation
	Death of Queen Caroline
	Visits Ireland
	Visits Hanover
1822	Visits Scotland
1823	Restores Windsor Castle
1827	Last visit to Brighton
	Death of heir presumptive, Duke of York
	Demolishes Carlton House
26 June 1830	Dies at Windsor Castle
	Succeeded by second brother, William, Duke of Clarence

PRINCE OF WALES

It was a German custom to supply food and drink to friends who came to inspect a new baby, and as George IV's mother was a princess of Mecklenburg-Strelitz, cake and alcoholic refreshments were duly provided for all those who called at St James's Palace to view her firstborn child. The bill came to £500, a sum that took a good deal of consuming in the eighteenth century. It was perhaps an augury of the profligate manner in which the boy would spend the greater part of his surprisingly long life.

George Augustus Frederick, the eldest son of George III and Queen Charlotte, was born on 12 August 1762. His father had succeeded his own grandfather, George II, two years earlier, and was now twenty-four years of age. George's mother was still only eighteen. By the time she was thirty-nine she would have given birth to an astonishing total of fifteen children, two of whom, both boys, died in infancy.

Almost immediately created Prince of Wales, George was just as instantly described as 'strong, large and pretty',[1] and strong, large and pretty he remained for many years, his rather florid good looks only fading as drink and drugs eventually wore away his initial stamina and pleasing physique. Pampered by a nursery staff under the management of Lady Charlotte Finch, the prince grew daily stronger, larger and prettier, and he also showed early signs of innate intelligence, supplying pert replies to questions about his health and learning to write by the age of five.

He had to wait only a year before he acquired a brother, Frederick, later created Duke of York, and of his fourteen siblings (eight brothers and six sisters) Frederick – not withstanding George's propensity to fall out with almost anybody – was the brother he loved. William, later Duke of Clarence and William IV, arrived in 1765; the first girl, Charlotte, created Princess Royal, a year later; and the very next year, 1767, Edward, Duke of Kent and father of the future Queen Victoria. The Prince of Wales's mother was almost permanently pregnant, and the lack of personal attention she was able to spare her enormous brood must account to some extent for the dissolute lives led by her sons. Although Frederick was their father's favourite and George was said to be their mother's, lacking what he may have considered sufficient maternal affection as a boy George became a spendthrift and a flamboyant, rather effeminate, dresser. Hopelessly immature in the expression of his affections as a young man, in middle age he chose the comforting and ample bosoms of matronly mistresses.

Unfortunately for George, he was saddled also with a less than satisfactory father. George's paternal grandfather, Frederick, Prince of Wales, had been the first civilised Hanoverian, a man who loved his children and treated them with every sign of affection. Tragically, he died when his eldest son, Prince George's father, was only twelve, and the future George III fell into the hands of incompetent tutors. Prince Frederick would never have dreamed of beating his sons; George III had Prince George and Prince Frederick soundly thrashed on the slightest pretext. Life at court was organised on lines so rigid that the king's daughters did not even address their father unless he spoke to them, nor were the queen's ladies-in-waiting ever permitted to sit. William Pitt, who became prime minister in

1783, was made to stand during an audience for two hours even though he suffered from gout. The Prince of Wales and his brother had plenty against which to rebel.[2]

Prince George was initially brought up at the Queen's House at Greenwich, built by Inigo Jones for the wife of Charles I, and at Richmond Lodge, a house at Kew formerly used by George II and Queen Caroline, for part of George III's complex character was attracted more to rural domesticity than to the grandeur of life in a metropolitan palace. But as the family grew larger almost annually, the king and queen required more spacious accommodation, and in 1772,[3] on the death of the king's mother, Princess Augusta, Dowager Princess of Wales, they moved into the White House, a property at Kew transformed in 1732 by William Kent into a commodious home for the late Prince Frederick. But even now there was not room for eight children and all their attendants, and George and Frederick, aged nine and eight respectively, were shunted off to the Dutch House nearby, the only royal residence at Kew still in existence today.[4]

Here the formal education of the princes got under way. The Earl of Holdernesse was appointed governor to the boys, but as Horace Walpole regarded him as 'a formal piece of dullness' it was just as well that ill health soon saw his departure for warmer climes, and the young princes came directly under the influence of a cultivated sub-governor, Leonard Smelt, and the newly consecrated Bishop of Chester, William Markham, appointed their Preceptor. Markham, whose pomposity was only alleviated by his learning, had previously been headmaster of Westminster and dean of Christ Church, Oxford.

Under the strict tutelage of these two, the Prince of Wales remained at his lessons until eight o'clock at night; it is no wonder that he gained an early inclination to keep late hours. Like any number of English monarchs, he never learned to spell, but he grew up with a grasp of the Classics and the royal necessity of speaking fluent French. Two cardinal virtues were urged upon him, to some extent in vain; to be truthful and to avoid flattery. His mother's specific advice, to 'abhor all vice', fell on totally deaf ears. She had little better success when she implored her son to display 'the highest love, affection and duty towards the King'.[5]

The Prince of Wales inherited his musical gifts and love of art from his grandfather, Prince Frederick, but his unfortunate libido from his father. He was also the unhappy recipient of a Hanoverian trait so marked as to be pathological: an inherent distrust and dislike of one's heir. George I had hated George II, and George II detested Prince Frederick. In the case of George III, he had an heir to the throne who appeared totally oblivious of his duty towards 'the Supreme Being' who had, his father continually reminded him, put him 'in an exalted station'.[6]

Despite an adolescent over-indulgence in food, and, contrary to his mother's wishes, a fondness for flattery, the Prince of Wales grew into a boy whom many people admired. A German member of the queen's household, Charlotte Albert, decided he had 'engaging and distinguished manners, added to an affectionate disposition'.[7] Frederica Planta, governess to the princesses, joined in the chorus of praise. She thought he was a fine boy with an open countenance and a manly air, and possessed 'the most obliging politeness, such as can only spring from goodness of heart'.[8] One of his amusing gifts, practised almost until the day he died, was for mimicry; he may not always have listened to what his ministers had to say, but he listened to how they said it, and on their departure he had his attendants in fits of laughter as he copied their mannerisms to perfection.

On the prince's own admission, as a young man he already had a penchant to grow fat, but as a Hanoverian he was full of Guelph genes. His hair was generally considered beautiful, his eyes clear blue, his nose 'a companionable one'.[9] He was agreeably self-mocking, and in a letter to one of his sisters' attendants he admitted he was rather too fond of wine and women, but in mitigation he claimed he never bore 'malice or rancour in his heart', which was true.[10]

However, there was not a single good feature in the prince's character visible to the king. When George was twelve his father had complained of his 'duplicity'. In adolescence, the king alleged, Prince George showed a marked lack of interest in German and history. As for the absence of any comprehensive knowledge of the Constitutions, laws or finances of European countries, only one crime merited harsher denunciation, the boy's lack of gratitude to 'the Great Creator'. But what worried the king most of all was that the prince's 'love of dissipation' had been 'trumpeted in the public papers'. Some of those with whom George had been cavorting were gamblers and drunkards; others were women. One, perhaps the first woman with whom George went to bed, was the wife of a groom, 'a great slattern, and more low and vulgar than that class of people usually are'.[11]

The trouble was, George III was no stranger to scandal. His second brother, the Duke of Gloucester, five years younger than the king (their mother had produced children in almost as rapid succession as Queen Charlotte was to do), had made a secret marriage in 1766, when he was twenty-three, to an illegitimate daughter of Sir Edward Walpole.[12] He was banned from court and spent half his time in Italy, the other half of it in the pages of the English newspapers, where gossip about his sexual adventures was reported. The king's third brother, upon whom he had conferred the dukedom of Cumberland, committed adultery with the Countess of Grosvenor, whose husband demanded £10,000 by way of compensation. In 1771 he did something much worse, he married a commoner, a woman, according to George IV's biographer Christopher Hibbert, 'much given to jokes and banter of unparalleled coarseness'.[13]

The king had had enough, and in 1772 he introduced into parliament the Royal Marriages Act, forbidding members of the royal family in direct succession to the throne to marry under the age of twenty-five without the consent of the sovereign, and over the age of twenty-five, if consent was still withheld by the sovereign, only with the approval of both houses of parliament. The Act is still in force today, and the first person to fall foul of it was to be the king's eldest son.

The Prince of Wales was only ten when the Royal Marriages Act was passed, but by the time he was seventeen he was quite old enough, and sufficiently well versed in British constitutional affairs, to know that while his father reigned it would be impossible for him to contract a legal marriage without consent. He admitted as much when in 1779 he was pouring out heartfelt expressions of love to Mary Hamilton, one of his mother's maids of honour. She was clearly a level-headed girl, who implored the prince to offer her no more than friendship, to stop sending her presents and to desist from his latest vice, that of swearing. Frustrated, George soon dropped Miss Hamilton for Mary Robinson, by general consent a woman with few virtues but abundant charms.

By the time Mrs Robinson met the prince she had been married at fifteen, had spent time in prison for debt and had become a celebrated actress. On 3 December 1779 the Prince of Wales went to Drury Lane to see her as Perdita in Shakespeare's *The Winter's Tale*. He flirted with her in public and bombarded her with love letters. The loyal and wise Miss Hamilton warned him to be careful, but the idea of a fantastical love affair was more than the Prince of Wales could resist, and he even asked Mrs Robinson to come to his apartments in Buckingham House, previously the home of the Duke of Buckingham (now Buckingham Palace), disguised as a boy. Even she, eccentric as she was, shrunk from 'the indelicacy of such a step'.

A brief and furtive meeting eventually took place at Kew. And the longer the time before the consummation of his desires, the more driven to desperate measures the prince became. Eventually he offered Mrs Robinson £20,000 on his coming of age if she would quit the stage and agree to become his mistress. This offer, from a headstrong and irresponsible boy of seventeen, was rashly accepted by the adventurous 21-year-old. No attempt was made by the prince to conduct his affair with discretion, cartoons depicting the pair of them appeared in the shops, and at Ranelagh pleasure gardens Mrs Robinson was virtually mobbed.

No sooner had the Prince of Wales made his conquest than he tired of Mrs Robinson and began to make overtures to a divorcée. In Hyde Park he cut Mrs Robinson, who pleaded that thanks to the prince's empty promises she was now burdened with fresh debts. After much haggling, the prince was obliged to approach his father with his problems, and the king went cap in hand to the prime minister, Lord North, busy desperately striving to save the American colonies. Between them they settled £5,000 on Mrs Robinson, in addition to a pension of £500 a year for life.

It is small wonder the Prince of Wales went off the rails when young. His father continued to regiment his life with endless instructions: he was given details as to when and where he might have dinner parties; he was to inform the king if he was going to the opera; he was to seek permission to attend a ball, but on no account was he to go to a ball in a private house; and his appearance at a masquerade was absolutely forbidden. Attendance at church on Sunday and at the king's Drawing Rooms was to be obligatory. 'When I ride out of a morning I shall ever expect you to accompany me,' George III told his son. On other occasions he might ride without the king so long as he did so for exercise, 'not lounging about in Hyde Park'. The king admitted he could 'reason more coolly on paper than in conversation', and ended by assuring the prince he wished to have him as a friend.[14] But Prince George found his father a difficult person to converse with, for the king hated to hear any opinion other than his own. Conducting a reasonable discussion was a form of intercourse quite alien to the king's nature.

No sooner had the Prince of Wales received these paternal instructions than he was struck dumb – quite literally, apparently – on parting from his beloved brother Frederick, who was being packed off to Hanover, the German Electorate ceded to the British crown on the accession of George I, in order to improve his knowledge of the German language. And three weeks later he lost his equerry, Lt-Col Gerard Lake, at thirty-six a valued mentor who was now posted to the lamentable war in America. 'Our parting,' Prince George told Frederick, 'as you may suppose, was a very severe trial to us both, especially as we had received so great a shock in our late separation from you. You know how much I loved him.'[15]

Both Colonel Lake and Prince Frederick endeavoured to offer sound advice to the Prince of Wales; Frederick, writing from Hanover, beseeched him to be 'upon as good a footing as possible with the King'.[16] But the prince complained that the king was always so 'excessively cross, ill-tempered and uncommonly grumpy', not to mention 'stingy'. He thought the 'unkind behaviour' of both his parents 'hardly bearable'.[17]

And so, instead of taking genteel exercise in Hyde Park the Prince of Wales deliberately rode 'like a madman', and at both Ranelagh and Vauxhall pleasure gardens he fell about the worse for drink. Prince Frederick wrote to warn his brother to take care of his health; the king claimed he was only an affectionate father 'trying to save his son from perdition'.[18]

The prince's bouts of drinking became so chronic he took to his bed to try to dry out. By now, too, numerous mature ladies were said to be receiving his favours. There was even talk of illegitimate children. By the time Prince George was twenty, Georgiana, Duchess of Devonshire, was describing him as 'inclined to be too fat' and looking 'too much like a woman in men's clothes'. But she admitted he was very handsome and good natured, although 'rather extravagant'. She thought he had an inclination to meddle in politics, and loved 'being of consequence'.[19]

The Prince of Wales's basic immaturity may be gauged by a letter he wrote to Prince Frederick after he fancied he had fallen in love with Countess von Hardenburg, wife of an aspiring Hanoverian envoy. 'O did you but know how I adore her,' he wrote, 'how I love her, how I would sacrifice every earthly thing to her; by Heavens I shall go distracted: my brain will split.'[20] The prince's brain was far more likely to split from a hangover than an excess of puppy dog devotion to a married woman. Prince George was a sensual youth, with all the emotional passion one associates with those who enjoy the visual arts, but as a sincere and monogamous lover he was not to be taken seriously. Even when the countess eventually yielded to the prince's wooing he felt it necessary to boast to Prince Frederick of 'the pleasures of Elysium'.[21]

The affair ended in high and rather absurd melodrama. Count Karl von Hardenburg discovered his wife's infidelity and wrote to the prince, who 'almost fell into fits' and asked the king's permission to go abroad, permission the king did not hesitate to refuse.[22] The countess suggested elopement, and although he felt tempted, the prince squiggled out of the situation by explaining that if he did elope he would be penniless. Then Prince George did what so many young men of his age, upbringing and muddleheadedness do, he ran to his mother for comfort, and then fainted. The queen 'cried excessively', quite possibly genuinely moved by her son's evident dependence on her after all.[23] As her duty dictated, she told the king what had happened, and keeping a cool head he sent for the count and gave orders that he and his wife were to leave for Hanover without delay.

TWO

PATRON OF THE ARTS

During the reigns of the first two Hanoverian monarchs, the king had supported one political party, the Prince of Wales another, the heir to the throne in effect acting as a rallying point for the opposition. Once again the pattern of strife was to be repeated. George III was a Tory, so Prince George threw in his lot with the Whigs – and they with him, for should the king die then patronage on a massive scale would be at the new king's disposal. The leader of the Whigs in parliament was a delightfully disreputable but brilliant orator, Charles James Fox, whose appetite for wine, women and conviviality matched precisely the tastes and habits of the Prince of Wales.

Fox's denunciation of the handling by Lord North of the War of American Independence eventually forced North, upon whom the king had daily depended for friendship and advice, from office, and in 1782 George III was compelled to accept Fox, aged thirty-three, as one of his Secretaries of State. A year later he was Foreign Secretary.

Fox began life immensely rich but lived, as did the Prince of Wales, permanently in debt; he was a compulsive gambler (the gaming table had a magnetic, and often fatal, attraction for many eighteenth-century men-about-town), who charmed the prince by his conversation and good nature, and whose scruffy appearance and contempt for convention found an echo in Prince George's desire to escape the enslavement of his father's court. As he approached his twenty-first birthday, the Prince of Wales was also enraptured by the prospect, held out to him by Fox, of receiving £100,000 a year with which to support his own establishment. The king was horrified, and thought £50,000 in addition to the revenues of the Duchy of Cornwall, which amounted annually to about £27,000, more than enough. After all, the prince was not even married.

That was a state of affairs soon to be altered, although in a most unsatisfactory manner. But first of all the prince required a London residence of his own. The king said he might have Carlton House, which stood on the south side of Pall Mall, on a site between what is now the lower end of Regent Street and the Duke of York's Steps. Built in 1709 for the Secretary of State, Henry Boyle, the house acquired its name when Boyle was raised to the peerage as Lord Carlton (sometimes spelt Carleton, and the house was spelt Carleton House as late as 1807). Boyle's heir was his nephew Richard Boyle, 3rd Earl of Burlington, the great patron of Palladian architecture, who inherited the house in 1725, making it over to his mother in 1731. A year later it was purchased, for £6,000, by Prince George's grandfather, Frederick, Prince of Wales.

It was a relatively modest town house, enhanced inside for Prince Frederick by William Kent, and out of doors by the creation of a much admired 12-acre garden. At first Frederick only intended Carlton House for purposes of entertaining, but eventually it became a principal home, retained until her death by his widow, Augusta. Prince George took one look at his late grandmother's London home and decided it simply would not do. What he, the Prince of Wales, required was a palace. So he instructed Henry Holland, the speculative builder of Cadogan Place and Sloane Street, to produce one.

An oblong hall was decorated with Ionic columns of brown Siena marble. Behind a music room was a Chinese-decorated drawing room, a foretaste of things to come in Brighton. In 1807 Carlton House had to be provided with a Gothic conservatory, and in 1813 John Nash added a stupendous Gothic dining room. The garden front soon rivalled that of Buckingham House, and the portico on the north front was as splendid as any wealthy country landowner had yet possessed. By 1819 there was a golden drawing room, a Gothic library, and even a throne room.

Unfortunately, the prince was quite incapable of affording such opulence. In the first six years unpaid bills mounted to £224,309. In desperation, the king asked parliament to underwrite these debts if the prince would promise 'to confine his future expenses'. Parliament knew that no such promise made by Prince George would be worth the paper it was written on, and the eventual outcome was an agreement to pay if the prince would oblige the country by getting married to Princess Caroline of Brunswick.

The horrors of such a misalliance lay some way in the future, however. For the moment, the prince was busily absorbed in importing craftsmen from France, searching dealers' shops for Dutch and English paintings, including some fine van Dycks, instructing agents overseas to purchase Sèvres china, Gobelin tapestries, candelabra, clocks, cabinets, bronzes. By 1789 the *New Town and Country Magazine* considered Carlton House 'a national ornament and the only habitable palace Great Britain can boast'.[1] But others were more critical; the architect Robert Smirke thought the apartments 'overdone with finery'.[2] Much influenced by Parisian taste and style, despite never having been to France, the Prince of Wales conceived a plan for Nash to construct a royal mile from Regent's Park to Carlton House, to be named Regent Street (this was during the years when he held the title Prince Regent).[3] But before the scheme could be completed the prince decided the Carlton House ceilings were too low, the air not good, his London neighbours too close for comfort; the house would have to be demolished and vast sums spent on turning Buckingham House into a London palace. And so in 1827 George had

Carlton House demolished. Not a brick remains, and on his grandfather's garden there arose Carlton House Terrace. The destruction of Carlton House was the one truly wicked act George IV committed.

On 11 November 1783 the Prince of Wales took his seat in the House of Lords. He did so as Duke of Cornwall. Just five weeks later his friend Charles Fox was dismissed by the king and at the age of twenty-four William Pitt, second son of the Earl of Chatham, became prime minister. Fox, however, again stood for parliament, and in 1784 he was returned for the Westminster constituency. Prince George made no secret of his support for the man the king had so recently removed from office, wore Fox's colours of buff and blue, and balanced on the garden wall of Devonshire House to cheer the triumphant candidate's procession. He gave a breakfast for Fox at Carlton House, and a second celebratory party that began at noon and went on all night.[4]

Totally excluded from affairs of state, and with nothing to occupy him but pleasure derived from horse racing, drinking and spending money, the Prince of Wales exhibited all the royal vices and a good many virtues. He was falling about drunk one minute, introducing classical quotations into his conversation the next. The musicologist Charles Burney, father of the diarist Fanny Burney, found he could discuss music with the prince for half an hour on end. Many other men of discernment, as dissimilar as the wealthy dilettante William Beckford and the staid and highly respectable Duke of Wellington, appreciated his charm, his wit, his excellent memory and of course his brilliant powers of mimicry. Lord Charlemont thought that if only the prince would drink in greater moderation he might well live to be a 'blessing'; Edmund Burke, who by and large found the prince's way of life disgusting, nevertheless believed he had it in him to become a great king.

The prince played the cello in the company of Haydn, and possessed a pleasant and well-trained tenor voice. He became a patron of Gainsborough, Romney and Stubbs. He was a reasonably good shot, a sturdy horseman, riding from London to Brighton and back again in ten hours, and his skill at four-in-hand driving was just as remarkable; he once covered 22 miles in a phaeton in two hours at a trot. In 1810 Oxford University conferred upon him an honorary doctorate of civil law in appreciation of his help in preserving an ancient library of papyri.

Had the king known the true reason why his eldest son was continually pestering him for permission to go abroad, in order, so he said, to escape his creditors and live more economically, relations would have been even colder than they already were. What Prince George really wanted to do was to pursue to the continent a lady he believed had given her promise to marry him.

She was a young widow called Maria Fitzherbert, whose arrival in London for the season in March 1784 was announced in the *Morning Herald*. Since the death of her second husband, Thomas Fitzherbert, Maria, who was very comfortably off, had been renting Marble Hall at Twickenham, the Palladian house George II had built for his mistress Henrietta Howard. But far from aping the manners of a mistress herself, Maria declined the Prince of Wales's advances. The granddaughter of a baronet, she happened also to be a Roman Catholic, and six years older than her royal admirer, who had first caught sight of her at the opera.

Not conventionally beautiful, Maria Fitzherbert nevertheless was renowned for her charm, her gracious conduct and her sympathetic ear. Needless to say, the more resistance Maria offered the more earnestly the prince beseeched her to succumb. Behaving like a neurotic hysteric, which was largely what he was, he threw himself into tantrums and swore, not too convincingly, that he would renounce the throne if only she would marry him.

Mrs Fitzherbert knew perfectly well that marriage was out of the question. The Royal Marriages Act of 1772 forbade the Prince of Wales to marry without his father's consent, which in any case would be automatically withheld if his intended bride was not a Protestant. So that was that – or it would have been under normal circumstances. But there was something distinctly abnormal about George IV, just as there was about his father, and a good many other Hanoverian forebears and future descendants. They suffered, to a greater or lesser extent, from an hereditary metabolic disorder known as porphyria, which in the case of George III eventually resulted in a state of mental derangement akin to clinical madness.[6]

Immature in so many ways, so liable to fall in and out of love at a moment's notice, at twenty-two the Prince of Wales, heir to the throne and to a brilliant future, announced that he was ready to marry a Catholic commoner with whom he could never hope to share the throne. At twenty-eight, twice married and far more level-headed, Maria Fitzherbert decided Prince George was too unreliable to make a satisfactory husband or protector, and prepared to retreat overseas. So the prince fell back on emotional blackmail. He stabbed himself.

Or at any rate, by the time Mrs Fitzherbert, chaperoned by the Duchess of Devonshire, arrived at Carlton House the prince was lying prostrate covered in blood, a reviving glass of brandy by his side. Some unkind people later came to believe the prince, having recently been bled by his doctor, had opened the wound and spattered blood about the place to make it look like attempted suicide. Overwhelmed by the bizarre situation in which she found herself, Mrs Fitzherbert weakly consented to marriage, the Duchess of Devonshire obligingly taking one of her own rings off to serve as an engagement ring.

Mrs Fitzherbert was right to maintain that a promise of marriage extracted under such conditions was void. Her immediate reaction, however, was to sail for France, and it was now that Prince George began his bogus requests to live abroad as well. Prevented by a firm refusal from 'his father and his Sovereign', Prince George besieged Mrs Fitzherbert with letters, one of them forty-two pages long. He addressed her as his wife, and protested that he would kill himself if they were to remain apart. Between bouts of letter-writing he would fall into 'hystericks', roll on the floor, tear his lovely hair out and make plans to elope to America.

It comes as no surprise to discover that while playing the role of a desolated lover the Prince of Wales was consoling himself with other women, and again drinking like a fish. Mrs Fitzherbert, for her part, appears to have been irresolute and therefore presumably attracted to the prince, for she meandered around the continent for a year before returning to England. 'I have told him I will be his,' she confessed to her companion Lady Anne Lindsay. But she added, 'I know I injure him and perhaps destroy forever my own tranquillity'.[7]

Afraid that if the prince married Mrs Fitzherbert he would forfeit his inheritance, and would therefore be in no position to patronise the Whig party, Fox advised him against such a rash course of action. Brazenly lying, the prince assured Fox there was not a shred of truth in reports that he was about to marry, and promptly set in train a hunt for a conspiratorial Anglican cleric to officiate. He alighted on the Reverend John Burt, currently languishing in the Fleet Prison. As Burt had gone to jail for debt he was easily persuaded to commit an act of felony under the Royal Marriages Act, the prince promising him an immediate £500 and a bishopric as soon as he came to the throne. Burt became a chaplain to Prince George but never a bishop, dying when he was only thirty.

Ten days before Christmas 1785, as dusk was closing in, the Prince of Wales arrived at Mrs Fitzherbert's London house, in Park Street, and entered the drawing room. Two witnesses were already present, an uncle of the bride and her younger brother. The brief ceremony over, this absurd charade descended into farce. On the way to Ormeley Lodge on Ham Common, where the honeymoon was to be spent, the prince's carriage broke down in thick snow, and he and Mrs Fitzherbert — and as such she continued to be known for the rest of her life — had to make their way on foot to an inn in Hammersmith for supper.

In the light of the marriage of George IV to Caroline of Brunswick ten years later, his liaison with Mrs Fitzherbert has ever since remained a matter of acute speculation; it certainly stands high in the catalogue of peculiar royal goings-on. But the facts seem fairly straightforward. A marriage service certainly took place, which was just as certainly illegal, and therefore invalid. The idea that Mrs Fitzherbert could believe herself validly married by an Anglican priest in itself defies belief, and both parties were well aware of the provisions and consequences of the Royal Marriages Act. Both were in effect tying a pretty knot to sanctify their relationship, which never could be other than that of clandestine lovers.

Perhaps the most famous of the many political satirists and cartoonists of the time, James Gillray, soon got down to work, and the prince and Mrs Fitzherbert became the subjects of ribald caricatures. Everyone in society appeared to know about the 'secret' marriage, and there was every danger of the subject coming up for discussion in parliament, for the prince's debts now amounted to the grand total of £269,878 6s 7¼d. Suggestions that his debts might be cleared if he married were countered by a declaration that he would never take a wife, and that he was quite happy for the crown to descend to children fathered by his brother Frederick.

Much given to dramatic gestures at the best of times, the prince now resolved to economise by shutting Carlton House, disbanding his racing stables and dismissing most of his staff and household. Leaving Mrs Fitzherbert to follow later, he took the public coach to Brighton, ostentatiously travelling on the outside like any gentleman too impoverished to possess transport of his own. It was not the prince's first visit to the small seaside town, formerly a fishing hamlet called Brighthelmstone. In 1765 his uncle, the Duke of Gloucester, had discovered the alleged benefits of bathing in the sea and drinking the spring waters at nearby Hove, and the Duke and Duchess of Cumberland had also spent several summers there, renting a property on the Steine called Grove House.

It was at Grove House that the Prince of Wales had stayed on his first visit in 1783, when bells had been rung and guns fired in honour of his august arrival. He attended the theatre in North Street and a ball in the Assembly Rooms at the Castle Inn, and it was to enjoy the pleasures of racing, bathing, and the informal life led at Grove House, that he returned the next year. By the time he was heading for the south downs in 1786, ostensibly to economise, he had already decided he must have a property of his own in Brighton.

He alighted on a modest farmhouse on the Steine, the property of Thomas Kemp, MP for Lewes. It was he who was to build the impressive Regency Kemp Town estate on the coast to the east of the Steine, comprising most importantly Lewes Crescent and Sussex Square, Chichester Terrace and Arundel Terrace, just a fraction of the architectural benefits brought to Brighton by the initial patronage of the Prince of Wales. In 1787, by which time parliament had obligingly agreed to pay off £161,000 of Prince George's debts, and to provide him with a further £60,000 with which to complete the additions to Carlton House, Henry Holland was summoned to Brighton, with orders to transform the prince's farmhouse into a Marine Pavilion.

Up went a small neo-classical house with a
central domed rotunda surrounded by Ionic
columns, and with bow-fronted wings enhanced by
a style of ironwork balcony so typical of Brighton
Regency houses. Within three years Brighton had
become, according to the *Brighton Directory*, one of
the most frequented and fashionable towns in
England. With the arrival later of a royal court,
elegant Regency squares and crescents proliferated,
and with the coming of the railway in the 1840s
Brighton's fortune was made.

Holland's Marine Pavilion consisted, on the
ground floor, only of a dining room, breakfast room
and library. And even after a new dining room and
conservatory had been added, stables for sixty
horses designed in the Indian fashion built between
1803 and 1808 dwarfed the prince's house. So in
1815, by which time the Prince of Wales was Prince
Regent, John Nash was called in. Over a period of
seven years were built the saloon, music room and
banqueting room, in which a chandelier weighing a
ton was hung, and the prince's symbols as a
freemason were incorporated in the decor.[8]

It was not until 1823 that the interior, with its
magnificent chinoiserie decoration, was completed,

but Grand Duke Nicholas of Russia was unlikely to have found anything amiss when in 1817 he sat down to a banquet comprising over 100 dishes. Oriental domes and minarets continued to spiral into the air, until by 1822 the exterior of the Royal Pavilion, as it is called today, with its power to enchant and startle, had come to its final fruition.[9]

T H R E E

POLITICAL ACTIVIST

Mrs Fitzherbert was installed in a villa only a moment's walk from the Prince of Wales's new Brighton residence, and in addition to the cost of his own building plans he spent £50,000 on gifts of silver, furniture and jewellery for her. Once the prince had set her up in a new London establishment as well, close to Carlton House, she began to entertain on a scale expected of a Princess of Wales. It would not have mattered how many houses the prince closed down in order to economise, it always seemed that another would inevitably be opened up.

But his generosity, if not on a scale to equal his personal extravagance, was nevertheless commendable. Fox's widow was to receive £500 a year; four illegitimate nephews £200 each. Many of his servants were provided for on retirement, and he even ordered that a pension should be paid to Flora Macdonald. He contributed £1,000 a year to the London poor and paid an annual subscription to a committee 'for bettering or abolishing the present disgraceful Trade by Chimney Sweepers'.

When the prince was still only twenty-six intimations suddenly arose that all financial worries might be swept away for ever. One autumn morning in 1788 the king sent for his doctor, Sir George Baker. He asked for opium, for he was suffering violent pain in his stomach. It was not the first such attack of pain the king had endured, but was by far the most severe. He also complained of cramp, rheumatism and a rash. Baker, who was as ignorant as the rest of his profession, prescribed castor oil and senna. The king's condition grew worse.

Throughout a concert at Windsor Castle the king spoke continually, changing the topic of conversation from moment to moment, and much to the consternation of both audience and artists he was seated one minute, standing the next. His sight began to fail, his memory became more and more muddled. But he remained sane enough to fear that he was going mad. On 30 October the Prince of Wales arrived at Windsor, which seemed to please the king. But at dinner six days later the king suddenly grabbed hold of the prince and hurled him against the wall. The queen had hysterics; the prince burst into tears. The king's distressing symptoms began to resemble more and more those of a man suffering from senile dementia; he would speak nonsense for hours on end, and sometimes, quite unlike his normal self, he would resort to indecencies. He bestowed honours on anyone who approached him. He believed London to be flooded. Hanover, he declared, was easily discernable through a telescope. Orders were issued indiscriminately, dispatches dictated to imaginary potentates.

The king's doctor became nearly as distracted as his patient, and further advice was sought. In mid-November Prince George asked the prime minister, William Pitt, to attend him at Windsor and discuss the crisis, for it was rumoured in London that the king's death was imminent, and that if he did not die, then he would be certified insane and a Regency declared. Dr Richard Warren, a physician summoned by the prince, told Pitt that the king was mad, perhaps because he hoped to profit under the prince if the king was declared unfit to rule. On the other hand, Sir Lucas Pepys, the fifth doctor to be called in, assured Fanny Burney, Keeper of the Wardrobe, that the king would 'certainly recover, though not immediately'.[1] Pitt's doctor also thought the king would recover.

Those doctors who remained pessimistic received hate mail. The king's popularity soared. The value of stocks and shares fell. On 27 November the Prince of Wales took it upon himself to call a cabinet meeting at Windsor to approve removal of the king to Kew. After putting up violent opposition to the idea, the king was eventually driven off with an escort of cavalry. At Kew he was denied access to his wife and daughters, and subjected, to all intents and purposes, to torture.

George III, even when the stability of his mind was being questioned, was a quick-witted monarch. Paid a visit at Kew by an unqualified quack called Francis Willis, who admitted to the king that he was really in Holy Orders, the king told him, 'I am sorry for it. You have quitted a profession I have always loved, and you have embraced one I most heartily detest.'

'Sir,' replied Dr Willis, 'Our Saviour Himself went about healing the sick.'

'Yes,' said the king, 'but He had not £700 a year for it.'[2]

Willis was an evil man, who told the king he was mad and that if he did not behave himself he would be put in a straitjacket. It was no idle threat. Willis and his two sons subjected the king to every imaginable indignity. Meanwhile, at Windsor, the Prince of Wales was strutting around as if already Regent, issuing orders, so Fanny Burney recorded, 'without any consideration or regard for his mother's feelings'.[3] When not at Windsor he was at Carlton House, giving grand dinner parties and drawing up a provisional list of posts to be offered to his Whig friends when his father died.

London was divided over the merits of their future sovereign. Some demanded to know whether the Prince of Wales was a papist or merely married to one, and they hoped that if he did become Regent he would forsake the gaming table and the turf. Whig pamphlets, of course, sang the prince's praises, describing him as a genius. The medical opinions of the king's fractious attendants were freely aired in parliament, as were the opinions of those who believed the eldest son and heir of the sovereign merely had a claim on the Regency, and of those who thought he had an inherent right. Pitt believed that parliament could choose a Regent; Fox declared that Prince George was the automatic choice.

Those who supported the Prince of Wales in this unseemly squabble wore 'regency caps' decorated with the prince's feathers. Prince Frederick, since November 1784 Duke of York, assumed he would soon be Commander-in-Chief, and it was confidently predicted that Mrs Fitzherbert was about to be made a duchess. The prince deluged the playwright and politician Richard Sheridan with letters, demanding to know the strength of his support. He discovered the answer when the government won a vote on the Regency by a majority of 64; it was the view of parliament that the prince enjoyed no inherent right to the Regency, and that if he was nominated, his powers of patronage should be strictly limited. But even before the prince had had time to lick his wounds the Regency Bill, passed on 12 February 1789, was hastily shelved. Having the previous year informed his fifth brother, Prince Augustus, aged sixteen, that their father was 'a complete lunatick',[4] Prince George now hastened to Kew to congratulate the king on his recovery. For almost a fortnight, however, neither he nor the Duke of York were permitted to see the king, for fear of a regal relapse. When a date was finally set for a reunion, George and Frederick were so frightened of the reception they feared they might receive that they arrived two hours late.

Part of the rivalry, and hence antagonism, between George and his parents was quite simply political. Tory slogans adorned a supper party at Windsor. When someone shouted 'God bless Pitt' as the prince drove by in his carriage, he let down the window and bellowed back 'Fox for ever!' A service of thanksgiving for the king's return to health was held at St Paul's Cathedral on 23 April 1789 when Pitt was loudly cheered, Fox as heartily hissed. As Fox's most illustrious supporter, the prince found himself the recipient of jeers and catcalls too.

But the prince gained plaudits when on 31 May 1792 he made his maiden speech in the House of Lords, just a few weeks short of his thirtieth birthday. It seems he only decided to speak on the spur of the moment, which would indicate that he spoke without notes, and he took the opportunity to affirm his attachment to the principles of England's 'great and sacred' Constitution, which to his dying day he would 'glory in professing'. He was only too well aware of the dangers of Republicanism; Paris was by now a bloodbath, and when the revolutionary government declared war on England the following year, Prince George reminded the Duke of York that the 'very existence of every Prince' depended on the 'total annihilation of this banditti'.[5]

But not even the French Revolution could distract the Prince of Wales from financial concerns. When York made a prosperous marriage (to Princess Frederica of Prussia), Prince George's recollections of the vows he had exchanged with Maria Fitzherbert began to fade. His stables alone were costing £30,000 a year, and Carlton House and the Marine Pavilion at Brighton were consuming money on an alarming scale. He had foolishly made attempts to borrow money in Holland, to be redeemable on his father's death. Thomas Coutts, whose bank was to receive royal accounts into the twentieth century, lent the prince £60,000. A further £20,000 was squeezed out of the duc d'Orléans. Prince George even asked his newly married brother to see whether his 'beau père', the King of Prussia, would 'do a little something in the loan-way'.[6] But by borrowing money all the prince was doing was falling deeper and deeper into debt. And his debts were already exorbitant. He owed his coachmaker £32,777. Tailors' bills amounted to £31,919. Once again he tried to retrench – by closing Carlton House and selling his beloved horses. But with tradesmen actually importuning him in the street with unpaid bills in their hands he realised there was only one solution – to follow the example of his brother, and marry.

His affection for Mrs Fitzherbert, and hers for him, had been cooling anyway. A wife would bring a dowry, and encourage parliament to vote him a decent income. And a marriage of convenience would still leave him free to enjoy amours, even if his girth was no longer that of an agile youth; by 1797 his weight was to reach a preposterous 17½ stone. Someone whose favours he briefly enjoyed was an actress called Anna Maria Crouch, born in 1763 and whose tomb, in the graveyard of St Nicholas Church, the original parish church of Brighthelmstone, is engraved with one of the most memorable epitaphs to be found in any church in England:

> She combined with the purest tastes as a Singer the most elegant Simplicity as an Actress: Beautiful almost beyond parallel in her Person, She was distinguished by the powers of her mind: they enabled her, when She had quitted the Stage, to gladden life by the charms of her conversation and refine it by her manners.

The Prince of Wales no doubt saw Mrs Crouch as Polly Peachum in the *Beggar's Opera*. Two other remarkable women known to the Prince of Wales are buried at this fourteenth-century church, dedicated to St Nicholas of Myra, the patron saint of fishermen. Perhaps the most remarkable is Phoebe Hessel, born in Stepney in 1713, during the reign of Queen Anne. She served as a private in the 5th Regiment of Foot, and actually fought at the Battle of Fontenoy under George IV's belligerent great-uncle and godfather, 'Butcher' Cumberland. Dying in 1821, she just scraped into the reign of George IV, who granted her a pension.

Nearby lies Martha Gunn, 'Peculiarly Distinguished as a bather in this town nearly 70 years'. Martha Gunn died in 1815, at the age of eighty-eight, having on many occasions assisted the Prince of Wales to step gingerly from her wheeled bathing hut into the briny. George's Shampooing Surgeon, Sake Deen Mohomed, who introduced Turkish baths to England and died aged 102, is also buried in St Nicholas churchyard.[7]

The first really serious contender for the Prince of Wales's affections, as far as Mrs Fitzherbert was concerned, was his first mistress of any consequence, the Countess of Jersey. The daughter of a bishop and mother of nine children, some already married, Lady Jersey was nine years older than the prince, and with her maturity and ready-made family she can justly be regarded as not only a sexual partner but also a source of maternal affection. She was, in fact, the first of three stately, aristocratic, matriarchal substitutes for the wayward affections of Queen Charlotte. Lady Jersey managed to convince the prince that the sole cause of his unpopularity was his liaison with a Roman Catholic, and once in love, the prince was prepared to believe anything. Equally in character, he was loath to lose Mrs Fitzherbert's company, and for a time he tried to run both women in tandem.

Maria Fitzherbert's position was further undermined, and the way made clear for the Prince of Wales to sort out his finances, when the Court of Privileges ruled that a secret marriage made between Prince Augustus and Lady Augusta Murray – made, that is to say, without the king's consent – was null and void. Lady Augusta was at least a Protestant. What hope had Mrs Fitzherbert, a Roman Catholic, of ever being accepted as the lawful wife of the heir to the throne? It was Prince George's cue to attend upon his father at Weymouth, where he was on holiday, and to inform the king that he had finally broken off relations with Mrs Fitzherbert (no mention was made of Lady Jersey), was prepared to live a respectable life, was ready, indeed, to marry.

Prince George's choice of bride, in so far as he actually made a choice, was to prove disastrous. The myriad ducal courts of Germany were the customary hunting grounds for royal brides, and in Brunswick there happened to reside a headstrong princess, Caroline, whose mother was the eldest child of Frederick, Prince of Wales, sister to George III and Prince George's aunt. Hence George and Caroline were first cousins. Such close kinship, however, was considered a minor detail in comparison to the young princess's unfortunate reputation; 'exceedingly loose', 'indelicate' and 'indiscreet' were some of the more polite descriptions she had acquired. There was also the matter of her personal hygiene. Not to put too fine a point on it, she was smelly.

Two of Caroline's brothers were said to be mad, and there can be little doubt that Caroline herself, like her cousin Prince George, had inherited some measure of porphyria. Yet although as a general rule the king was averse to marriage between first cousins, he told Pitt he gave his approbation. Someone else who eagerly encouraged the match was Lady Jersey. What had she to fear from a creature of whom it was said she had an indifferent character and not a very inviting appearance? The Earl of Malmesbury, previously Sir James Harris, was dispatched to Brunswick to inspect the young lady, a diplomatic mission fraught with possible comebacks. He found her head too big for her body, her neck too dumpy, her teeth only tolerable and going bad, her eyelashes white. But he decided she had fine eyes, good hands and attractive, abundant hair. Caroline's father warned King

George's emissary that his daughter, although not stupid, had no judgement, and it certainly seems that at twenty-four she had received scant training in etiquette.

A Marriage Treaty was signed on 3 December 1794, but severe weather and fighting on the continent delayed Princess Caroline's arrival in England until the following spring, when she had to endure the humiliation of being met at Greenwich by Lady Jersey, whom the king had appointed one of her ladies-in-waiting. They drove to St James's Palace where, quite needlessly, for they were upon an equal footing, Caroline attempted to curtsey to the Prince of Wales, whose own conduct boded ill. Retiring to a corner of the room he called Lord Malmesbury over. 'Harris,' he said, 'I am not well. Pray get me a glass of brandy.'

Malmesbury foolishly advised water, so the prince strode off to report his first, unfavourable impressions of Caroline to the queen. 'My God! Does the Prince always act like this?' the astonished Princess Caroline asked Lord Malmesbury, speaking in French, for her English was almost non-existent and presumably Lord

Malmesbury did not speak German. 'I think he's very fat,' she added, 'and nothing like as handsome as his portrait.'

Could any marriage have got off to a more unpromising start? At dinner things only got worse. Most probably jolted into action by nerves, the princess rattled away, much of her conversation consisting of vulgar jokes at Lady Jersey's expense. The countess remained aloof; the prince just looked disgusted. As princesses spurned by their husbands are apt to do, Caroline lost no time eliciting the sympathy of the public, actually making a speech from an open window, conduct unheard of for a female of any royal family. As though to keep open an avenue of escape, the Prince of Wales had already arranged for Mrs Fitzherbert to receive £3,000 a year, and he had also asked his friends to continue to show her due respect and honour. Now he wrote to say she was the only woman he would ever love. Interestingly, Mrs Fitzherbert never referred to Princess Caroline as the Princess of Wales.

Royal weddings traditionally took place in the evening, and it was on the evening of 8 April 1795, in the Chapel Royal at St James's Palace, that

George and Caroline were most unhappily wed. The princess was given away by Prince George's second brother, William, Duke of Clarence, and was attended by the daughters of two dukes and two earls. The Prince of Wales was supported by the Dukes of Bedford and Roxburghe, both bachelors. This time he had helped himself to the brandy, rather too liberally, and the Duke of Bedford had some difficulty in keeping the prince on his feet. It seemed quite obvious that the Archbishop of Canterbury, John Moore, suspected a previous entanglement, for when he asked if there was any lawful impediment to the marriage he 'laid down the book and looked earnestly at the King, as well as at the bridegroom'.[8] Lord Melbourne, the father of Queen Victoria's first prime minister, recorded that the 'prince was like a man doing a thing in desperation; it was like Macbeth going to execution; and he was quite drunk.'[9]

After the ceremony the Prince of Wales conducted his bride to a Drawing Room in almost total silence. She, however, smiled and nodded to everyone she passed, and seemed perfectly happy, which was just as well, for as the evening wore on the prince became drunker than ever, and when eventually he braced himself to enter Princess Caroline's bedroom he fell in a stupor into the fireplace. And there he lay for the rest of the night.

Karl Anton's portrait of Charles James Fox, the genial, disreputable but brilliant Whig politician for whom in 1784 George IV, as Prince of Wales, did not hesitate to canvas. The death of Fox in 1806 was a severe personal and political blow to the prince. (By courtesy of the National Portrait Gallery, London)

Sir Joshua Reynolds' portrait of the twice widowed Maria Fitzherbert, at the age of thirty-two, the long-suffering mistress with whom George IV went through an illegal and invalid marriage ceremony in 1785. (By courtesy of the National Portrait Gallery, London)

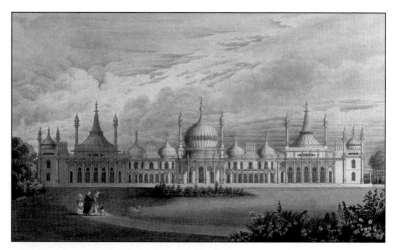

In 1815 John Nash was called in to transform the Prince of Wales's Marine Pavilion at Brighton, which had begun life thirty years previously as a modest farmhouse. In 1850 the Royal Pavilion was sold by Queen Victoria to Brighton Corporation.
(Royal Pavilion, Brighton)

The Banqueting Room at the Royal Pavilion, designed by Robert Jones. The chandelier weighs a ton. (Royal Pavilion, Brighton)

Henry Holland's imposing Corinthian portico built for Carlton House, the Prince of Wales's sumptuous London residence in Pall Mall, illustrated in W.H. Pyne's *Royal Residences*. In 1827, three years before his death, George IV had the house, built at colossal expense, pulled down. (Guildhall Library, Corporation of London)

George Cruikshank's none too flattering depiction of George IV as Prince Regent, the title he was granted in 1811, at the age of fifty-one. (© The British Museum)

Caroline of Brunswick, cousin of George IV and from 1795 to 1821 his wife, in a portrait by Sir Thomas Lawrence. The marriage was a disaster, but resulted in the birth of a daughter, Princess Charlotte, who died in childbirth. (By courtesy of the National Portrait Gallery, London)

The Marchioness of Hertford, painted by Reynolds. She supplanted the Countess of Jersey in the affections of the Prince of Wales in 1806. Five years older than the prince, married and rich, Lady Hertford was one of a succession of mature mistresses who satisfied the prince's need for maternal love. (Leeds Museums and Galleries, Temple Newsam House: photograph Courtauld Institute of Art)

George IV once covered 22 miles in a phaeton in two hours at a trot. Here he is depicted driving a phaeton in an engraving by J. Dickinson. (The Royal Collection © 1998 Her Majesty The Queen)

The sensation of 1820, the year of George IV's accession to the throne, was the trial of the queen. Her daily visits to the House of Lords to listen to the evidence provided much amusement and excitement for Londoners, many of whom, because her husband was so unpopular, took her side. (Royal Pavilion, Brighton)

Installation of a Knight Companion of the Bath.

While she received the copious shower, | And grew from that auspicious hour
He got a step in honor's Path . | A Knight Companion of the Bath.

Queen Caroline's scandalous conduct overseas led in 1820 to a Bill of Pains and Penalties being introduced in the House of Lords accusing her of adultery, a treasonable offence. Her chamberlain, Bertolommeo Pergami, was widely believed to be her lover, and was satirised as a Knight Companion of the Bath. (University of Reading)

George IV's over-indulgence in food and drink resulted in his weight at one time reaching 17½ stone, a gift for a Regency satirist like James Gillray, who showed him up as 'A Voluptory under the Horrors of Digestion'. (By courtesy of the National Portrait Gallery, London)

The wealthy Marchioness of Conyngham, who became mistress to George IV in 1820, painted by Sir Thomas Lawrence, an artist who was commissioned by the king to provide a gallery of other portraits for the Waterloo Chamber at Windsor Castle. (Private Collection, now destroyed: photograph Courtauld Institute of Art)

FOUR

THE AMIABLE HOST

Oddly enough, the early months of Prince George's marriage to Caroline of Brunswick struck observers, in particular his bevy of affectionate sisters, as perfectly amicable, and we know, short as the marriage in any true sense turned out to be, that at least it was consummated, for on 7 January 1796 the Princess of Wales gave birth to a daughter. Baptised Charlotte, no doubt in honour of her paternal grandmother, the baby princess was next in line to the throne after the Prince of Wales.

But George and Caroline were basically incompatible, and in any case, the Prince of Wales had no intention of giving up Lady Jersey. In consequence, Prince George was vilified in the press while the princess was applauded on her appearance at the opera, and trumpeted by the *True*

Briton as 'the object of so much unmerited ill treatment'. Such a description contrasted more than somewhat with the prince's belief that his wife was the 'vilest wretch this world was ever cursed with'.[1] Capable of working himself up into an hysterical passion at the best of times, the prince came firmly to believe his wife posed a threat to the very existence of the monarchy.

Within three days of his daughter's birth the Prince of Wales also came to believe he was about to die, a condition he anticipated several times before the actual event took place. So despite his protested illness he concocted a 3,000-word will, leaving his child to the protection of the king and queen. To his 'beloved and adored Maria Fitzherbert' he bequeathed every scrap of property he possessed. He expressed a wish to be buried with 'as little pomp as possible', but with a picture of 'the wife of his heart and soul' in the coffin with him. After her own death, it was his desire that Mrs Fitzherbert should be interred with him. Out of childish spite he left the person 'who is called the Princess of Wales' one shilling.

Needless to say the prince did not die; he was not even ill, unless perhaps in the head, and in a futile attempt to patch up his marriage to Princess Caroline it was agreed that Lady Jersey should no longer serve as a lady-in-waiting. Caroline, who was residing at Carlton House, went so far as to ask the prince's forgiveness 'if she had ever displeased him in the past'.[2] So Prince George paid a visit to Carlton House, but as soon as dinner was over he departed to enjoy the company of his mistress. At least two courtiers, the Duke of Leeds and Lord Thurlow, thought that 'the extraordinary way in which the Prince of Wales treated his wife could be attributed only to madness'.[3]

The single person to find the Princess of Wales totally unpalatable was her husband, who declared he would rather see toads and vipers crawling over his food than even sit at the same table as her. There were plenty of other men who found the princess's company agreeable enough, and some who even felt tempted to take advantage of her admittedly wanton conduct.

The irony of the situation was that not only had the Prince of Wales saddled himself with a wife he had so soon come to detest but the main purpose of the marriage, solvency, still eluded him. By 1795 the prince was in debt to the tune of £630,000. It would be a frightening sum today; at the time it represented a massive accumulation of unpaid bills. In October that year the king's state coach was stoned, and cries of 'Down with George!' greeted his arrival at the House of Lords, for the ghastly marriage of the heir to the throne had indeed come to taint the institution of the monarchy. The person held responsible, however, was not Princess Caroline but Prince George himself.

Fickle in his affections as ever, the Prince of Wales discarded Lady Jersey and sought a reunion with Mrs Fitzherbert, whose secret marriage was declared valid in 1800 by the Pope. That was sufficient for the prince to announce that Roman Catholicism was the 'only religion for a gentleman',[4] and for Mrs Fitzherbert to host a 'public breakfast' for 400 guests. They gathered at two o'clock in the afternoon and sat down to dinner at seven, and it was not until five o'clock the following morning that the party broke up.

What Prince George sought above all was cosy domesticity, and his wild extravagance was a way of holding his boredom at bay. Mrs Fitzherbert now told Lord Stourton that she and the Prince were 'extremely poor but as merry as crickets',[5] and to

Lady Anne Lindsay she confided that they lived 'like brother and sister'.[6] Their alleged poverty was, of course, relative. The prince allowed Mrs Fitzherbert £4,000 a year, she paid £6,000 for a new London house, and methods of economising involved dismissing members of the household who had never been paid, and keeping the salaries of others five years in arrears. But economies there had to be. How else was the prince to afford two dozen waistcoats at a time, or seventy-four pairs of gloves? Or, come to that, thirty-six toothbrushes instead of one – or thirty-two walking sticks when perhaps a couple would have sufficed?

While the king commonly dined on mutton and stewed pears, the Prince of Wales thought nothing of running up monthly bills of £500 for groceries, £1,000 for wine. He was attended by forty indoor servants, including no fewer than seven pages. Had he already been crowned he could not have lived in greater regal splendour.

The reason the prince was bored was that the king consistently denied him employment. In 1797 George III had said 'No' to his eldest son becoming Lord Lieutenant of Ireland. Twice when invasion from France seemed a distinct possibility the prince begged in vain for a senior army command, and it rankled that he was merely a colonel of dragoons while his brother, the Duke of York, had been made a field marshal. But in 1801 it seemed as though full-time employment might at last materialise. The king suffered an appalling relapse.

As before, George III was confined at Kew, again tortured by his cruel and stupid doctors. And once again the Prince of Wales leapt into action, summoning Pitt, who had resigned as prime minister at the start of the new year, and his successor Henry Addington, to Carlton House. But a new maturity seemed evident. The prince got on well with Addington, who rose high in the prince's estimation when he proposed that he should receive an additional £60,000 a year for three years to help pay off his debts. But politically the prince's position was difficult. He toyed with new administrations, but he was unable to discover the truth about his father's condition, and until the king was officially declared unfit to rule the prince was unable to control events. The king's condition disconcertingly wavered between lucidity and lunacy.

The prince continued to entertain members of the opposition, much of the entertainment consisting of a monologue delivered by the host. The member of parliament for Thetford, Thomas Creevey, an industrious diarist, recalled that during one dinner the prince 'was very gracious, funny and agreeable, but after dinner he took to making speeches, and was very prosy as well as highly injudicious. He made a long harangue in favour of the Catholics and took occasion to tell us that his brother, William, and himself were the only two of his family who were not *Germans*.'[7]

George IV had nothing if not a vivid imagination. He later came to believe he had fought at the Battle of Waterloo and led a charge at Salamanca.

Caught in a good light, the Prince of Wales could bowl over most people with his charm and courtesy. The assistant governess to his daughter, Princess Charlotte, said she had never met anyone with 'such captivating manners'.[8] Unfortunately the same could not be said of the Princess of Wales, who was now living in garish luxury at Montague House, Blackheath. It was commonly reported that she liked nothing better than to entertain young men in private, to sit on the floor while exchanging scandal with her ladies-in-waiting and to eat raw onions and swig ale. Rumours of affairs were rife;

one with George Canning was widely believed, and there were tales that she was the mother of at least one illegitimate child. Unfortunately for even an estranged Princess of Wales, adultery constituted an act of high treason.

By 1806 both the Prince of Wales and the king reluctantly agreed that an investigation into the princess's conduct should be held, and a Commission of Enquiry was duly set up. Conflicting evidence was heard from courtiers and servants alike, yet the Commission made the astonishing assertion that the allegations of misconduct ought to be believed until some 'decisive contradiction' was received. This was sufficient for the Prince of Wales to convince himself he had a case for divorce, but although the king accepted that his niece and daughter-in-law had been guilty of much 'levity and profligacy'[9] it also had to be accepted that no actual proof of adultery had materialised.

The investigation into the Princess of Wales coincided with an increase in the prince's political influence. Pitt, who had been recalled as prime minister in 1804, died in 1806 and his successor, Lord Grenville, a Whig, insisted on the prince's great friend Charles Fox being appointed Foreign

Secretary. Thomas Creevey, perhaps sarcastically, noted that the prince had begun to be 'a very great politician' and 'considered himself at the head of the Whig party'.[10] Nevertheless, the prince complained that he had not been sufficiently consulted over the new ministerial appointments – not that it was as yet his prerogative to be consulted at all. But many now recognised that with so many of the prince's friends in office, and the king's health so permanently precarious, power had shifted decisively from the Court of St James's to Carlton House.

Indeed, the prince was beginning to act as though already head of state, recommending peerages and baronetcies with indecent insistence. Not to be outdone in the political stakes, Princess Caroline openly supported the Tories. In effect, three courts now vied for attention: the king's, the Prince of Wales's and the Princess of Wales's. The issue over which they fought was the Commission of Enquiry. The king said he would be guided by the Cabinet; the prince demanded a divorce; the princess, justice.

The Cabinet fudged the issue, telling the king it was up to him whether or not he continued to receive the princess. This was not good enough for the king, who informed the Cabinet he wanted more definite advice. While the politicians continued to debate the matter, farce took over from scandal, for it was now alleged that the princess had dispatched, in a box and via a third party, a gift to one of her lovers of a lock of pubic hair.

Frustrated by insolvency and the Cabinet's refusal to endorse his demands for a divorce, the Prince of Wales was finally deflated, in September 1806, by the death of Fox, followed by the fall of the Whig ministry. He declared himself from now on politically neutral.

Many Tory friends of Princess Caroline entered government under the premiership of the Duke of Portland.[11] Not only did the new Cabinet endorse advice to the king to receive the princess, they agreed to her request for accommodation at Kensington Palace. Once an apartment at St James's Palace fell vacant, she was to have that as well. Her rehabilitation was well under way, and all the prince could do was continue to insist at least on a formal separation; and to insist with urgency, so that he could not be held responsible for his wife's ever mounting debts. He also dreaded the possibility of Caroline claiming her right to be crowned when eventually he became king.

One reason the prince spent so much time at the Pavilion in Brighton was that his patronage of the town had brought the population up to 7,000, with a consequent increase in building and trade. And in Brighton he was seen as a splendid adornment to the place, an acknowledged patron of the arts, a jovial benefactor, a popular local squire. At the Pavilion, so Thomas Creevey recorded, the prince was 'always merry and full of his jokes'.[12] Lady Jerningham told her daughter, 'It is really not to be described how amiably polite and fascinating his manners are on his own ground – the most finished civility joined to the utmost degree of good-natured affability'.[13]

After dinner, served at 6.00 p.m., the prince would sometimes adjourn, a little unsteadily, to the Assembly Rooms. Here the guests would scramble for a good vantage point from which to witness the arrival of Prinny, as he was commonly called. If a visit to the Assembly Rooms was not on the cards, then Mrs Fitzherbert would play at cards at the Pavilion while the Prince of Wales discussed the progress of the war with France, called upon his organist, Charles Wesley, to perform, sang a lusty song himself or sat on a sofa tapping his foot in time with the music. Precisely at midnight the band packed up and in were wheeled sandwiches and more wine.

Always late to bed, the prince was a notoriously late riser, but once dressed and coiffed he could rely, in Brighton, on a seemly progress along the Steine, where deferential townspeople would not have dreamed of shouting the sort of insults that came as second nature to the London mob. His guests included the brilliant and delightful Richard Sheridan, who played endless pranks on the other guests, and kept everyone laughing. The arbiter of fashion, Beau Brummell, who taught the prince the correct way to take snuff, was another favoured friend.

At Brighton, George was, of course, well out of the way of his tiresome wife, edging her way ever closer to the neighbourhood of Carlton House. He was also further removed from the tantrums of his ill-bred daughter, being brought up with her own household in her own home, Warwick House. With parents who were first cousins and both tainted

with unstable Hanoverian genes, it was small
wonder that Princess Charlotte showed so many
symptoms of serious maladjustment. She was vain,
imperious, impetuous and ill mannered. Prince
George blamed these defects on her mother, who in
point of fact had been forbidden to see Princess
Charlotte other than on formal visits to Windsor
Castle. Prince George took no pleasure in his
daughter's company, preferring to dote, in
Brighton, upon the charms of a child called Minny
Seymour, the orphaned daughter of Lord Hugh and
Lady Horatia Seymour. She had been adopted by
Mrs Fitzherbert, and upon this delightful little girl,
whom he treated with loving indulgence, the prince
offered to settle £10,000.

It was Minny Seymour's aunt, the Marchioness
of Hertford, who was to become the Prince of
Wales's next motherly mistress. Lady Hertford was
rich, and she and her husband, a former
ambassador to Berlin and appointed Master of the
Horse in 1804, shared the prince's pleasure in
French furniture, large quantities of which filled
Hertford House, their London home in Manchester
Square. Lord Holland thought Lady Hertford
'stately, formal and insipid',[14] so that she presented

just the sort of challenge that would appeal to the Prince of Wales's almost masochistic list of attributes in a woman he desired to conquer. She was also not far off fifty, and as Lady Stafford icily commented, 'elderly dames' seemed 'to be his taste'.[15]

The prince was still only forty-four, and once again proved himself capable of pining with love for a woman who held out against him. He wrote copious letters to Lady Hertford, ran a fever and lost his appetite. He insisted on being blooded, and if a doctor was not on hand to perform the operation he had no hesitation in lancing a vein himself. Laudanum was his medicinal remedy for all attacks of illness brought on by emotional anxiety.

Eventually, Prince George made a complete fool of himself by laying siege to Lady Bessborough, already happily fixed up with a lover, Lord Granville Leveson-Gower, to whom Lady Bessborough reported the grotesque scene, the prince kissing her neck, sobbing, pledging vows of eternal love, one moment on the couch, the next on the carpet. So ill-directed were his emotions that while using Lady Bessborough as a surrogate for Lady Hertford, he was imploring Mrs Fitzherbert to return to him after she had decided to leave the field clear for her new rival.

The prince's indiscriminate need for love was all of a piece with his magpie instinct for acquiring possessions. Had he received one iota of parental affection as a boy he might not have been such a wretchedly unhappy man. But with the death in 1810 of the king's favourite daughter, Princess Amelia, and the profound shock it caused the king, it became increasingly apparent that before too long the Prince of Wales would at least have a definite purpose in life. George III now failed to recognise people; his conversation had become 'unconnected' and obscene; he was seventy-two and almost blind. All that delayed the passing of a Regency Bill was the fear of Tory politicians that they would be dismissed by the Prince of Wales if he came to power.

But with perfect propriety the prince declined to discuss politics with anyone, and awaited the decisions of his father's ministers. Lord Holland thought Prince George's behaviour exemplary; that he had conducted himself with 'great caution, great dignity and great feeling'.[16] But – as in 1789 – a severely restricted Regency was proposed. The prince summoned all his brothers to Carlton House, and the result was a letter signed by the Duke of York to the prime minister, since December 1809 Spencer Perceval, complaining of a situation 'perfectly unconstitutional'.

With so much uncertainty as to whether once again the king might recover his wits, and a Regency of any kind last only a matter of months, Prinny caved in, agreeing to a restricted Regency for the first year. At midday on 5 February 1811 a contingent of Grenadier Guards arrived at Carlton House. Yeoman of the Guard took up their stations; so did the Life Guards. Members of the Privy Council began to arrive, and the Prince of Wales made his way to the grand saloon to receive them, with, so the newspapers dutifully reported, 'the most dignified and graceful deportment'. It would have been too much to expect a Hanoverian to invite his heir to attend such an historic occasion, so Princess Charlotte was obliged to peep through the window from the garden as her father took the oath as Regent of the United Kingdom of Great Britain and Ireland.

REGENT

The first thing the Prince of Wales did on becoming Regent was to promote himself to the rank of field marshal. Then he gave a party, inviting 2,000 people – some of them dead, as it turned out – to a fête at Carlton House. Vast quantities of food and champagne were supplied, and when Prince George himself sat down to eat in the Gothic conservatory he did so in the company of half the French royal family. His mother, however, stayed away, distressed at such merry-making during the 'great calamity' of the king's continued ill health.

Absent also, on the orders of the queen, were the prince's aging spinster sisters. Not surprisingly, Princess Caroline did not receive an invitation, but with great good humour she provided new dresses for those of her ladies who had been asked.

Another absentee was Princess Charlotte, now fifteen and still as awkward in her deportment and as assertively talkative as ever. She had been packed off to Windsor. Mrs Fitzherbert had declined to attend if Lady Hertford, and not she, was placed at the Regent's table, and from the moment of the Regency this faithful, devoted and long-suffering mistress never spoke to Prince George again.[1]

Notwithstanding the celebratory mood, the newly installed Regent struck some of those who worked with him on state papers as very nervous about discharging his duties, a nervousness not infrequently relieved by recourse to 'the liquor chest'. Constitutionally he was free to dismiss and construct administrations whenever he chose. He had inherited a Tory government, and it was generally assumed their services would be dispensed with, and the Whigs, whom previously the Regent had so openly supported, be invited to take their place.

But the Regent was basically lazy, and had a strong aversion to change. Once in power he proved less of a radical than in the past, and began to fear that the Whigs wanted reform on too sweeping a scale. By the autumn of 1811 he had escaped to Brighton, leaving both his ministers and his political worries in London. 'God bless you all!' he would say to his guests, with a gracious wave of his hand, as he departed for bed. On 31 October Thomas Creevey arrived at the Pavilion to find the Regent 'in the best humour', looking 'uncommonly well, though very fat'. Five years ago, Creevey had recalled, 'when he was first in love with Lady Hertford, I have seen the tears run down his cheeks at dinner, and he has been dumb for hours, but now that he has the weight of the Empire upon him, he is quite alive'.[2]

The Regent's good spirits were brought down again at a ball given for Princess Charlotte by the Duke and Duchess of York, when he put on a sprightly demonstration of a Highland fling, slipped and fell. Every three hours, to relieve the pain, he took 100 drops of laudanum. It seems the injury to his ankle, superficial in itself, had triggered a recurrence of symptoms akin to those that plagued his father. 'What will become of us,' Lady Bessborough wailed, 'if as well as our King our Regent goes mad? It will be a new case in the annals of history.'[3]

Once recovered sufficiently to meddle in politics again, the Prince Regent – the title by which he was known for the next nine years – displayed one of his major failings, indecision. He would ask advice and then seek advice about the advice he had been given, and in attempts to form some sort of coalition all he succeeded in doing was offend his former Whig supporters.

From an international point of view, the madness of George III and his replacement as king in all but name by the future George IV, could not have occurred at a more inopportune time; England was entering the last phases of a life and death struggle with the usurper of the French throne, Napoleon. In 1805 the prince had wept over the death of England's greatest sailor, Vice Admiral Nelson; since then the Tories were considered to have done rather well over their management of the fighting in the Peninsula, but the great decisive battle of Waterloo still lay on the bloody horizon. European politics were in turmoil, and steady, consistent government was called for. Unfortunately, by nature George was a ditherer.

Creevey went so far in his rage at the Regent's apparent betrayal of the Whigs as to describe him as 'doomed, from his personal character alone, to shake the throne'.[4] It was not thought at all odd until well into the reign of Queen Victoria for the monarch to take sides politically, but during a banquet at Carlton House the Regent turned his verbal guns on the Whigs with such violence he reduced his daughter to tears.

Through no fault of his own, the Prince Regent now managed to lose his prime minister. Spencer Perceval was shot in the lobby of the House of Commons by a deranged man who had been ruined by the war. The Regent replaced Perceval with Lord Liverpool, but then he came up against the bugbear of eighteenth- and nineteenth-century politics; no sooner had the Regent filled one post than someone said they would refuse to work with so-and-so; on this occasion, Canning refused to join the government if it meant working with Castlereagh. Then Lord Wellesley, the brother of the Duke of Wellington, declined office because he wanted to hold himself in readiness to take over as premier.

Everything collapsed anyway when Liverpool's administration lost a vote of confidence and had to resign. No wonder Sheridan thought the Regent 'in a state of agitation beyond description'.[5] To make matters worse, the Regent became a butt of ridicule in the *Examiner*, whose editor, John Hunt, and his brother Leigh, author of the offending article, ended up under arrest with 'intention to traduce and villify his Royal Highness the Prince of Wales, Regent of the United Kingdom'. They were both fined £500 and sent to prison for two years.

Charles Lamb came to the convicts' rescue with a poem titled 'The Prince of Whales.' It began:

> Not a fatter fish than he
> Flounders round the polar sea.

This may have been the quip that gave Beau Brummell his parting shot when the prince fell out with him, speaking to Lord Alvanley at a ball but cutting Brummell. 'Alvanley,' Brummell called out, 'who is your fat friend?'

Yet the Regent had a gift for flattery, which he exercised to considerable effect on Byron. His favourite authors, however, remained Walter Scott and Jane Austen. He could hold his own in conversation with the formidable Madame de Staël, and could charm an attentive hostess like the wife of the Bishop of Lincoln, who had been advised by a member of Princess Charlotte's household, 'The more you are dressed the better, certainly with diamonds'. Pages of instructions ended on a reassuring note: 'He will make all easy for you; he is so well bred.'[6] He made it all so easy for his hostess that she reported to her sister 'his correctness here [at Buckden Palace] was perfect'. Yet within days of returning home he was dead drunk.

He sobered up sufficiently to take part in the victory celebrations that followed Napoleon's abdication. 'Our Prince Regent is never so happy as in show and state,' Lady Vernon noted, 'and there he shines incomparably.'[7]

What it seems he could never escape were domestic embarrassments. Lady Elizabeth Foster, who married the Duke of Devonshire when he was widowed, believed that for the past 'seven or ten years' there had been general agreement about the 'imprudence of conduct, indelicacy of manner and conversation, and criminal attachments' of the Princess of Wales,[8] and in 1813 the Privy Council confirmed that 'intercourse' between the princess and her daughter was to be subject to 'regulation and restraint'.[9] Not that this worried Caroline or Princess Charlotte; there was little love lost between them.

What now nearly gave the Prince Regent a heart attack was his daughter's unwise encouragement of a young army captain, Charles Hesse, an intrigue apparently encouraged by the Princess of Wales, who would lock them in a bedroom at Kensington Palace saying, 'A present je vous laisse, amusez vous.'

Charlotte confessed to her father, who forgave her but made immediate plans to have her safely married. His choice of bridegroom fell, for no very obvious reason, on Prince William of Orange. Unfortunately, Princess Charlotte thought him ugly, but after a time she changed her mind, and they became engaged. Negotiations broke down, however, when the House of Orange insisted that the heir presumptive to the throne of Great Britain should live at The Hague, and Princess Charlotte stuck her heels in and declined to leave England.

With plans for the nuptials well advanced, Princess Charlotte found a good excuse for breaking off the engagement when she learned the Princess of Wales was not to be invited to her wedding. It was with 'astonishment, grief and concern' that the Regent received a letter from

Warwick House informing him his daughter's engagement was 'totally and for ever at an end'.[10]

As though to goad her father, who most of her life had ignored her, Princess Charlotte now took to entertaining a succession of European princes without a chaperone present. Among them was Prince Leopold, who had fought with the Russian army against Napoleon. He was merely the third son of an unimportant duke – of Saxe-Coburg-Saalfeld – and had his way to make in the world. Marriage to the heir to the British throne would be a glittering prize.

The possibility of her parents divorcing had always held a serious threat to Charlotte, for if the Regent divorced he would be free to marry again, and might produce a male heir. Hence she had dissuaded her mother from going abroad, for she felt sure that such a move would prove the prelude to divorce, and the possible loss of her inheritance.

Such a loss would have caused no great inconvenience to the country. Charlotte was ill educated and not very bright. Informed of her indiscreet flirtations at Warwick House, the Prince Regent, accompanied by a fresh entourage of lady companions to replace those who had failed to keep proper vigilance over his daughter, marched as fast as his gout would allow him from Carlton House to Warwick House, stormed upstairs and informed Princess Charlotte her ineffectual ladies were to be dismissed and she herself confined to Carlton House for five days and then removed to Cranbourne Lodge at Windsor; there she was to suffer virtual house arrest.

As adept at creating drama as her father, the princess managed to slip away, ran as far as Charing Cross, jumped into a hackney coach and offered the driver a guinea to take her to her mother's house in Connaught Place. As her mother had gone to Blackheath for the day, Charlotte ordered dinner.

There then ensued an unseemly fiasco; as messages were dispatched stating the princess's terms for returning home, the Lord Chancellor was left sitting in his carriage and Lord Ellenborough arrived armed with a writ of habeas corpus. Others who turned up to argue, reason and take sides included the Dukes of York and Sussex.[11]

By the early hours Henry Brougham, no friend to the Prince Regent, had persuaded the princess that if she held out against her father and appealed to the people there would be bloodshed, and she would be held responsible. Insisting she would never marry anyone under duress, she gave in and went to live at Windsor, where her new ladies kept a strict eye on her. She was forbidden to write letters, receive visitors or attend social engagements except her grandmother's musical entertainments at Frogmore. The final blow to her morale was news that her mother was definitely planning to go abroad.

In August 1814 the Princess of Wales, travelling under the name of Countess Wolfenbüttel,[12] accompanied by her daughter's former paramour, Captain Hesse, and a young doctor called Henry Holland, later the son-in-law of the Reverend Sydney Smith and said to be 'unfit to attend a sick cat', embarked at Worthing. There was to be no divorce, but the princess's itinerant trip landed her, six years later, on trial for treason.

In June the following year the Regent became the focal point of the sort of theatrical scene dear to his heart. Major the Hon. Henry Percy burst in upon a party in St James's Square, still bespattered with blood and mud, to surrender to the Prince Regent the French colours captured at Waterloo and to announce a glorious victory. 'I congratulate you,

Colonel Percy,' the Regent said. Alas, little of the credit rubbed off on him; the London poor had more pressing matters on their mind, like the 1815 Corn Law.

The Prince Regent gradually came to realise that no set of restrictions on her freedom would encourage Princess Charlotte to exchange the ennui of Windsor for Prince William of Orange, and although he regarded Prince Leopold as ambitious, he agreed to his daughter's marriage to him. Leopold was poor and of no political consequence, but at least he was a man of honour, brave, good-looking if stiff, and the princess appeared to be in love with him. Consent was formally granted during an amicable family gathering in Brighton, an allowance of £60,000 a year was settled on the couple, and it was agreed they should live at Marlborough House when in London; a wealthy member of parliament bought Claremont Park at Esher for £69,000, and made them a gift of that too. The Regent wanted to confer upon Leopold the dukedom of Kendal, which would have entitled him to a seat in the House of Lords, but this was believed at the time 'inconvenient, personally, to the Consort of the future Queen'.[13]

Charlotte's childhood had not been a happy one, and with her husband she began to settle into more peaceful ways. 'My mother was bad,' she told Prince Leopold's doctor, Christian Stockmar, 'but she would not have become so bad as she was if my father had not been infinitely worse.'[14] But she was now reconciled to her father. Her mother she was never to see again.

Ominously, Princess Charlotte twice miscarried. When for a third time she conceived she was attended by a more than usually incompetent doctor, Sir Richard Croft. On 3 November 1817, at Claremont, she went into labour for fifty hours. 'Nothing can be going on better,' Sir Richard informed Prince Leopold's equerry, having denied food to the princess and declined help from two other practitioners. At nine o'clock on the evening of 4 November the princess was delivered of 'a beautiful fine boy'.[15] Unfortunately, he was dead.

Later that night the princess was seized by pain. The ever resourceful Croft poured brandy and wine down her throat until she complained he had made her tipsy. The pain spread from her stomach to her chest. She could scarcely breathe. Convulsions followed. She could not speak, but seemed more composed. And then, without a struggle, she died.

With magnificent generosity the Prince Regent exonerated Croft from all blame. His reputation, however, was in ruins, and on 13 February 1818, while attending another patient whose difficulties in childbirth appeared to resemble those of Princess Charlotte's, Croft reached for a pistol conveniently hanging on the wall and shot himself.

Prince Leopold, having lost both his wife and son, was grief stricken. It is harder to judge the Regent's true feelings, for he was so prone to emotional over-reaction. There can never have been any very serious possibility of him producing another child, and now his brother, the Duke of York, was heir presumptive. But York also was childless, and likely to remain so. Next came the Duke of Clarence. He had ten children, all illegitimate, the offspring of his mistress, the charming actress Mrs Jordan, from whom he had precipitately separated in 1811. The Duke of Kent remained unmarried, also content with a mistress. The thought of the Duke of Cumberland, married since 1815 and undeniably mad, ascending the throne did not bear thinking about. Sussex was a bachelor. So, at this time, was the Duke of Cambridge. A scramble for the throne was on.

KING

A missile of some sort – quite possibly a bullet from an air-gun – went whistling past the Prince Regent's face as his carriage was driven down Pall Mall. He was constantly hissed and booed, for while farmers and tradespeople struggled to make a living he continued to give balls at Carlton House. A general stampede towards the altar by members of his family did little to calm the general mood, especially as his brothers had dual motives: to produce an heir to the throne and to persuade parliament to provide an increased income.

The Duke of Clarence's matrimonial enterprises reduced almost everyone to despair. Surely no prince can ever have chalked up such a list of rejections. Having received the thumbs down from two heiresses, the daughter of an earl and the widow of a duke, he set his sights on the sister of the Tsar. When the government declined to pay his expenses so that he could pop over to Russia to court her, the Regent gave him £1,000. It was money down the drain.

He tried an English princess; then the eldest daughter of the Landgrave of Hesse. She refused, so the duke, wonderfully unaware of his inadequacies as a dashing suitor, turned his attentions to the eldest daughter of the Electoral Prince of Hesse-Cassel. In desperation the Regent suggested his brother go to Denmark, but the year 1818 found Clarence back on home ground. He had proposed to 'a fine vulgar miss', Miss Wyckham by name, due to inherit an Oxfordshire estate. 'On this being told to the Regent, his Royal Highness *groaned*.' It was, according to Lady Jerningham, 'his way of disapproving'.[1]

Finally, the Duke of Clarence won the hand of the 25-year-old Princess Adelaide, eldest daughter of the Duke of Saxe-Coburg Meiningen. The diarist Charles Greville thought her 'frightful, very ugly, with a horrid complexion'.[2] They were married at Kew on 11 July 1818, kept company by the Duke of Kent, who had landed up with a young widow, Princess Victoria, the sister of Prince Leopold.[3]

Valiant efforts by the future Queen Adelaide failed to produce the longed-for heir. A little girl, born in 1818 and baptised Charlotte, only lived a few hours. In 1819 the Duchess of Clarence miscarried, but in 1820 she again gave birth to a daughter, Princess Elizabeth. Born six weeks premature, at four months Elizabeth died. Two years later the duchess again miscarried, losing twins.

Meanwhile, on 24 May 1819, at Kensington Palace, the new Duchess of Kent gave birth to a daughter. The Regent stood as godfather, and after much indecision and argument at the font, instigated by himself, the child was named Alexandrina Victoria. As Queen Victoria, she was destined to reign for sixty-three years.[4]

In 1820 the childless Duchess of York died, and it was always possible that the duke might marry again and produce an heir to take precedence over any nieces or nephews. With the birth in December the same year of the Duchess of Clarence's daughter, Elizabeth, Princess Victoria of Kent found herself for four months only fifth in line of succession. When he was widowed at fifty-seven, George IV might conceivably have married again, and under all the circumstances it was almost by chance that Victoria ever became queen, not least because the

monarchy had never been so unpopular. Lady
Hertford was nearly tipped out of her sedan chair
and had to be rescued by Bow Street Runners; 1819
saw the massacre by soldiers of peaceful protesters
in a field at Manchester.

On the royal family's domestic front the one
glimmer of light was the much improved relations
between the Prince Regent and his mother. When
work on the Brighton Pavilion ground to a halt
through lack of funds, Queen Charlotte gave her
son £50,000, and she threw a party for him at the
Queen's House, as the former Buckingham House
was known – not, she explained, 'à la manière de
Carlton House, but about 150 or 200 people'. She
added: 'If you would like to take a quiet dinner
with me en famille I will order it at six that we may
have a little time to breathe before the company
comes.'[5]

Queen Charlotte died at the Dutch House, the
house where the Regent had been educated, on 17
November 1818, with her eldest son holding her
hand. Perhaps with some slight exaggeration, when
Princess Elizabeth wrote to her brother to
commiserate, she told him, 'No parent was ever
more wrapt up in a child than she was in you, and I

firmly believe that she would with pleasure have sacrificed her life for you'.[6]

Where the Regent's relations with his estranged wife were concerned, matters were going from very bad to absolutely impossible. While gallivanting round the continent the Princess of Wales was said to have 'dressed almost naked' and to have danced with her servants. It was generally assumed, largely on account of their irregular sleeping arrangements, that the princess's *valet de place*, Bertolommeo Pergami, swiftly promoted chamberlain, was her lover. Deserted by most of her English suite, she was now attended by some 200 disreputable hangers-on, and on a flamboyant pilgrimage to the Holy Land she had ostentatiously ridden into Jerusalem on an ass.

In 1818 two lawyers and an army officer were sent to Milan to make official enquiries about the princess's conduct. Eighty-five people were examined, and the Milan Commission concluded the princess was guilty of adultery. The question of what to do about it was brought to a head by the death, on 29 January 1820, of George III. Two days later George IV emerged from Carlton House to hear the proclamation of his accession read, caught a severe chill and nearly died himself.

He spent part of his convalescence reading books in the library to try to discover a precedent for excluding his wife's name from the liturgy. The government obliged by agreeing that Queen Caroline should be neither prayed for nor crowned. But they drew the line at divorce, upon which the king was equally determined, and in his frustration he lost his temper with the prime minister, Lord Liverpool, with the Duke of Wellington and the Lord Chancellor. What also irked him was the government's determination not to increase the civil list now that he was king.

He soon learned a lesson in nineteenth-century kingship, however. Thinking the solution was to sack his ministry and ask Lord Sidmouth to form a new administration more amenable to his wishes, George IV was made to realise that no responsible politician would accept office under such circumstances, and he was obliged to climb down, if only in his own inimitable fashion.

He wrote to Liverpool:

The King is fully sensible of the importance of publick economy and is desirous to make every personal sacrifice on his part for that object, and the

King will never require that the intended arrange-
ment shall be disturbed unless it shall be found to be
inconsistent with the dignity and splendour of the
Crown which the King considers to be inseparable
from the public interest.'[7]

So far as the queen was concerned, the king and
his government now resorted to bribery. They
offered Queen Caroline £50,000 a year if she would
relinquish her title and remain abroad. But brazen as
ever she set off for Calais, having written to Lord
Liverpool to ask for a yacht to convey her to
England and requesting, at the same time, in her
fractured English, 'to be informed of his Majeste's
intentions what residence should be allotted to me,
either phermenent or temprory'. Hopelessly
gauche too, but perhaps wanting to stake her claim,
she signed the letter 'Caroline Queen of England'.

In the event, the 'Queen of England' landed at
Dover from the ordinary packet. *The Times*, echoing
its proprietor's political sympathies, hailed her as a
brave woman. A royal salute was fired from the
castle (she was, after all, queen consort), and the
next day substantial crowds turned out to cheer her.
By midsummer 1820 the queen was installed at

Brandenburg House in Hammersmith, a house built by Prince Rupert of the Rhine for one of his mistresses.

On 5 July a Bill of Pains and Penalties, technically a private Bill enabling the queen to be tried without recourse to the courts, was introduced into the House of Lords. It accused Caroline of adultery and sought to deprive her of her title and to dissolve her marriage.

London was galvanised. Satirists flourished. The enquiry (although almost invariably referred to as a trial, the queen was never strictly speaking on trial) began on 17 August. Unless armed with good excuses, peers were compelled to attend, unlike the queen herself; but she would not have missed the excitement for anything, and duly showed up in their lordships' chamber. But the novelty soon paled. In a room provided for her retirement the queen played backgammon, and on one occasion, while she was in the chamber, she nodded off. Lord Holland seized the initiative:

Her conduct at present no censure affords
She sins not with couriers but sleeps with the Lords.

There were many who believed the queen to be mad – one such was Madame de Lieven – and increasingly it was felt that the distasteful proceedings were a mistake, with no guarantee that the Bill would pass. Reluctantly, Lord Grey thought the queen ought to be acquitted, if only as a matter of political expediency. On 6 November, when a vote was taken, the government's majority was a mere twenty-eight, tantamount to a moral victory for the queen. Four days later, on the third reading, the government's majority was down to nine.

By now the queen's advocates had obtained a copy of the will the king had made in which he referred to Mrs Fitzherbert as his wife, and matters looked like backfiring; surely if the king had been married to Mrs Fitzherbert he had no right to the throne? Lord Liverpool doubted whether the Bill would pass in the Commons, and abandoned it.

The queen had been vindicated. Bonfires were lit, church bells rung. It had been a grave defeat for the Tory party, who began to see a future liberalisation of their own policies as the only way to survive. As Christopher Hibbert has sagely noted, 'An age was dawning in which the Reform Bill could become a reality'.[8]

Amidst all this amazing confusion, preparations for the king's coronation, planned for 19 July 1821, were going ahead. He intended to follow the service favoured by James II, and the government provided £243,000 for the purpose, a sum which makes present-day expenditure on pageantry seem modest. The king's only concern was that the queen would try to interrupt the proceedings, which foolishly she did. But on turning up at Westminster Abbey uninvited she was politely but firmly shown the door.

Inside, the heat was so intense that on several occasions during the five hours of ceremonial the king, weighed down with robes 'of great size and richness', and wearing a heavy brown wig, seemed on the point of passing out. Revived by frequent sniffs of sal volatile, His Majesty eventually repaired to Westminster Hall to enjoy the last coronation banquet ever held. 'Of the splendour of the whole spectacle it is impossible for me to give you the *slightest* idea,' Lord Denbigh, the senior earl present, wrote to his mother.[9]

George IV was soon to have no need of a divorce. Quite suddenly, it seems, less than a month after the coronation, the queen was taken ill. On the evening of 8 August 1821 she died. It was with immense relief that the king learnt from her will that she had expressed a wish to be buried in Brunswick. So back to the German dukedom from which she had so rashly been summoned she duly returned.

With the death of Queen Charlotte and his own accession to the throne, George IV had found himself in possession of a fine town house, in addition to Carlton House, the Queen's House in Pimlico. Nash, he thought, was just the architect to turn the place into a palace fit for a king. Nash virtually rebuilt the house, round a three-sided courtyard, with its principal front of Bath stone overlooking the extensive gardens, newly landscaped by William Aiton. The cost amounted to some £600,000, and the result, not finished at the time of the king's death, was Buckingham Palace, the official London residence of the sovereign since the time of Queen Victoria.

George IV began his ten-year reign with a visit to Ireland, the first state visit to be paid to Ireland by a British monarch since the reign of Richard II. The passage to Dublin, in August 1821, 'was occupied in eating goose-pie and drinking whiskey', and the king arrived 'dead DRUNK'.[10] Ireland had much to commend it, but as far as the king was concerned what commended it most was the prospect of a stay at Slane Castle, the home of his new mistress, the Marchioness of Conyngham.

Lady Conyngham was fifty-two, fat, very, very rich and a grandmother – just the sort of cuddly matriarch to provide the king with another compliant husband and a ready-made family, a family, with the exception of the eldest son, who disapproved of his mother's liaison, whom he more or less adopted. The king flirted with Lady Conyngham outrageously, and gave her carte blanche to act as hostess in Brighton.

Returning from Ireland, to prepare for a visit to Hanover, George IV's ship ran into a terrifying storm. The tiller was lost and the ship was 'for some minutes down on her beam-ends', the king reported to the omnifarious Sir William Knighton. Only the 'undaunted presence of mind, perseverance, experience and courage' of the captain of the *Royal George*, Sir Charles Paget, 'preserved us from a watery grave'.[11]

Knighton was the man to whom the king was most closely attached, possibly because he was the repository of so many of the king's secrets. A doctor by profession, he received a baronetcy and served, unofficially, as a private secretary. He was loyal and discreet, and became, so the king informed him in 1821, his 'dearest and best of friends'. It was Knighton who now accompanied the king on his continental jaunt.

Embarking at Ramsgate, the king was welcomed at Calais by the duc d'Angoulême, and in Brussels he dined with the King and Queen of the Netherlands. Wellington showed him over the field of Waterloo, and then he set off for Osnabrück in the tracks of his great-grandfather George II, the last King of Hanover to visit the Electorate sixty-eight years previously.

Back in Brighton, the king became almost crippled with gout, drank copious quantities of cherry brandy, and lost his appetite both for food and work. Not that his appetite for work had ever been great, and now in order to get him to sign papers his ministers found the best method was to ask his valet to seize a favourable opportunity. Plunged into pessimism, the king spoke constantly of dying.

Yet his mood swings could take everyone by surprise. Asked to accept a cut in the civil list of

£30,000 a year he disappointed the opposition by happily giving his consent. What was always guaranteed to cheer him up was a children's party. He adored other people's children, and he was for ever buying them rocking-horses, dolls and lead soldiers.

A visit to Scotland planned for 1823 was brought forward a year, in a bid by Lord Liverpool to divert the king from a second continental trip, for fear he might get too enmeshed in foreign affairs. No reigning sovereign had been to Scotland since Charles II, so the king took the opportunity of spending a small fortune on costumes and adornments he thought appropriate. One coat was altered so frequently it eventually cost £600.

On 10 August 1822 the king boarded the *Royal George* at Greenwich, and four days later he arrived at Leith, in weather so wet Sir Walter Scott felt obliged to tell the king he felt 'perfectly ashamed'. His host at Dalkeith Palace was a lad of sixteen, who happened to be the Duke of Buccleuch and whose catering arrangements the king did not entirely trust, so he had his own staff take over the kitchen. He held a levee at Holyroodhouse attired in

Highland dress, and knighted the Scottish painter
Henry Raeburn.

For some time, Castlereagh had been showing
every sympton of a nervous breakdown, even telling
the king a fantastic rigmarole about being
prosecuted for homosexual offences, and it was
while in Edinburgh that George IV received the
shocking news that his foreign secretary had
committed suicide. The king wanted Wellington in
his place, but Lord Liverpool insisted on appointing
Canning, whom the king detested. The king said he
was prepared to dismiss the government and put in
the Whigs, but Wellington, a wise and relatively
disinterested statesman, gave him another valuable
constitutional lesson when he told him it was his
duty to accept the best man for the position.

In 1824, despite intermittent ill health and
appalling pain from gout (there were times when he
took to a wheelchair), the king caused work to begin
on his most important architectural achievement:
the modernisation, if not indeed the actual salvation,
of Windsor Castle. When George IV took up
temporary residence in 1823 he found he had
inherited a 700-year-old hotchpotch of small,
dissimilar rooms, often without proper connecting

corridors. Eight commissioners were appointed to investigate the situation, and the architect who obtained the plum job of restoration was Jeffry Wyatt. In 1824 parliament voted an initial £150,000, based on Wyatt's estimates, which proved hopelessly inadequate for the work that required to be carried out, and on 12 August that year, his sixty-second birthday, the king laid the first stone of the gateway named after him, giving access from the Upper Ward to the Home Park.

Fifty wagon loads of rotten timber were removed, houses in the precincts were pulled down, towers repaired – or in the case of the Brunswick Tower, completely rebuilt. Charles II's Baroque rooms along the North Terrace were transformed into State Apartments, and along the East Front were constructed a Grand Corridor and a series of superb drawing rooms for the private use of the monarch.[12] From every approach the skyline is dominated by the castellations of Jeffry Wyatt – or Wyatville as he later came to call himself. And although a distinguished librarian at Windsor, Sir Owen Morshead, thought the 'highly medieval machicolation would do credit to Hollywood', he had to admit that Wyatville (and

George IV, come to that) had found a workhouse and had left a palace.[13]

The king's other great achievement at Windsor had been to call in Nash to convert the Royal Lodge in the Great Park, for most of the twentieth century the Windsor residence of Queen Elizabeth the Queen Mother, into a charming Gothic *cottage orné*.

The king enhanced the Royal Collection, buying major works by Rubens and Rembrandt. He commissioned portraits from Thomas Lawrence for the Waterloo Chamber. To the British Museum he presented his father's library. He was instrumental in having the Stuart Papers edited and a biography written of Nelson, and the Royal Society of Literature owes its origins to him. He encouraged the idea of a national picture collection, and two years before his death the National Gallery in Trafalgar Square was opened.

And yet his own last years were incredibly sad. In 1827 his favourite brother, and his heir presumptive, the Duke of York, died. At his funeral in St George's Chapel it was so cold the dukes of Sussex, Wellington and Montrose all caught shocking colds, as did the Bishop of Lincoln, from which he died. And by now the king's days were spent almost in stupefaction. After breakfasting in bed and reading the newspapers he would doze off again, and seldom dressed before six o'clock in the evening.

One evening, according to the Duke of Wellington's great friend Mrs Arbuthnot, the king drank two glasses of hot ale, three glasses of claret and a glass of brandy, consuming at the same time some toast and strawberries. On another occasion, she reported, he was given physic, and then three glasses of port and a glass of brandy. She thought the mixture of ale and strawberries had been enough to kill a horse.

In 1829 Sir Walter Scott found the king at Windsor holding court in bed, wearing a white cotton nightcap and a dirty flannel jacket; he was sipping chocolate. There was a doctor in attendance, discussing the Windsor menagerie, and the Duke of Cumberland, talking about uniforms. When a page came in to announce that the prime minister had arrived the king got out of bed, put on a blue *douilette* and a black velvet cap with a gold tassel, and shuffled into the next room to receive him.

He had become breathless, and had begun to lose his sight. Always prone to melodrama, he repeatedly predicted he would 'be dead by Saturday'. But he reserved his most dramatic scene and his best lines to the last. In what became known as the Blue Room, where later both William IV and the Prince Consort were to die, the king spent his last night propped up in a chair. At about half-past three on the morning of 26 June 1830 he suddenly called out, 'Good God, what is this?' His page, Thomas Bachelor, ran across the room. The king clasped his hand. 'My boy,' he said, 'this is death.' And this time it was.

NOTES

CHAPTER ONE

1. Quoted in Christopher Hibbert, *George IV: Prince of Wales* (Longman, 1972), p. 1.

2. In *George IV* Hibbert makes the odd assertion, p. 4, that George III did not like Hampton Court and declined to live there because 'it brought him unwelcome memories of an unhappy childhood'. George III never lived at Hampton Court during his father's lifetime, and his childhood, certainly up to the age of twelve, when his father, Frederick, Prince of Wales, died, was blissfully happy.

3. Not 1771, Hibbert, *George IV*, p. 4.

4. The Dutch House, built in 1631 and sometimes called Kew Palace, is situated in Kew Gardens, and is open to the public.

5. Royal Archives, Windsor Castle.

6. Ibid.

7. Quoted in Hibbert, *George IV*, p. 9.

8. Royal Archives.

9. Lady Anne Lindsay, quoted in Hibbert, *George IV*, p. 10.

10. Ibid.

11. Hibbert, *George IV*, p. 12.

12. Not his eldest brother (Hibbert, *George IV*, p. 12), who was Edward, Duke of York and Albany.

13. Hibbert, *George IV*, p. 12.

14. Royal Archives.

15. Ibid.

16. Ibid.

17. Ibid.

18. Ibid.

19. Chatsworth MSS, Chatsworth, Derbyshire.

20. Royal Archives.

21. Ibid.
22. Ibid.
23. Ibid.

CHAPTER TWO

1. Patrick Montague-Smith and Hugh Montgomery-Massingberd, *The Country Life Book of Royal Palaces, Castles and Homes*, (Country Life Books, 1981), p. 108.

2. Hibbert, *George IV*, p. 35.

3. It was George IV who opened up a view of the park from the south front of Windsor Castle, continuing the Long Walk planted by Charles II to the gates of the castle itself. In 1831 he gave a focal point to the 3-mile vista by commissioning Richard Westmacott to execute a 26-foot high equestrian statue of George III, known as the Copper Horse.

4. An eighteenth-century 'breakfast' was not a 'working breakfast' such as politicians indulge in today. It was a major entertainment in someone's honour.

5. The Act of Settlement of 1701 decreed that the sovereign must be a communicant member of the Church of England. As a Roman Catholic consort would be required by the Roman Catholic Church to bring up his or her children in the Catholic faith, it follows that no member of the royal family in direct succession to the throne may marry a Roman Catholic without renouncing their right to the throne, which is what, in 1978, Prince Michael of Kent chose to do.

6. Porphyria can be traced in the British royal family back to Mary, Queen of Scots, and it is now generally accepted that four of George III's sons were sufferers. John Brooke presents modern medical findings in *King George III* (Constable, 1972).

7. Hibbert, *George IV*, p. 51.

8. The Prince of Wales was Grand Master of the Prince of Wales's Lodge, constituted in 1787.

9. George IV paid his last visit to the Royal Pavilion in 1827, three years before his death. The Pavilion was inherited first by William IV, and on his death in 1837 by Queen Victoria, who made occasional visits during the first eight years of her reign but sold it

in 1850 to Brighton Corporation. During the First World War the Pavilion was used as a hospital, and in 1920 the first of the original contents to be returned were handed over by Queen Mary. Restoration work had proceeded in various stages over a period of 100 years when in 1975 a catastrophic arson attack caused severe damage to the music room, the room in which, in 1823, Rossini had performed. In recent years the gardens have been re-landscaped; the stables were long ago transformed into a concert hall, library and museum; and today the Pavilion, fully restored, can be viewed in all its redecorated and refurnished Regency splendour.

CHAPTER THREE

1. Hibbert, *George IV*, p. 83.
2. Hibbert, *George IV*, p. 86.
3. Hibbert, *George IV*, p. 88.
4. Royal Archives.
5. Ibid.
6. Ibid.
7. The Church of St Nicholas, in which Dr Johnson and Wellington, when a boy, used to worship, contains a font made about 1160 from a single piece of Caen stone. For many years the church had uninterrupted views out to sea, and served as a welcome landmark for sailors.
8. Hibbert, *George IV*, p. 147.
9. Queen Victoria's journal, Royal Archives, 13 November 1838. The story had been related by the 1st Viscount Melbourne to his son, who passed it on to Queen Victoria. King Leopold of the Belgians, briefly the son-in-law of George IV, also told Queen Victoria her uncle had been '*extremely* drunk', but his information, although no doubt accurate, must have been second-hand.

CHAPTER FOUR

1. Royal Archives.
2. Ibid.
3. Hibbert, *George IV*, p. 160.
4. *The Times*, 4 July 1800.

5.   Hibbert, *George IV*, p. 173.

6.   Ibid.

7.   Hibbert, *George IV*, p. 195.

8.   Hibbert, *George IV*, p. 201.

9.   Hibbert, *George IV*, p. 219.

10.   Hibbert, *George IV*, p. 220.

11.   The 3rd Marquess of Salisbury, who became prime minister for a second time in 1895, was the last peer to hold that office. It has ever since been regarded as essential that the prime minister should be available to answer personally to the House of Commons; hence in 1963 the 14th Earl of Home placed his peerage in abeyance for his lifetime in order to become leader of the Conservative Party.

12.   Hibbert, *George IV*, p. 232.

13.   Ibid.

14.   Hibbert, *George IV*, p. 248.

15.   Ibid.

16.   Hibbert, *George IV*, p. 274.

CHAPTER FIVE

1.   Mrs Fitzherbert was supplied with a generous pension; £6,000 a year until George IV's accession in 1820, when it was increased to £8,000 a year, and after his death in 1830 her allowance was raised by William IV to £10,000 a year. William even made an illuminating inference to her marriage to George IV by permitting her servants to wear the royal livery.

2.   Christopher Hibbert, *George IV: Regent and King* (Allen Lane, 1975), pp. 8–9.

3.   Hibbert, *George IV: Regent*, p. 13.

4.   Hibbert, *George IV: Regent*, p. 19.

5.   Hibbert, *George IV: Regent*, p. 21.

6.   Hibbert, *George IV: Regent*, p. 27.

7.   Hibbert, *George IV: Regent*, p. 31.

8.   Hibbert, *George IV: Regent*, pp. 38–9.

9.   *Annual Register*, 1813.

10.   Royal Archives. Prince William of Orange eventually married Grand Duchess Anna, sister of the Tsar.

11.   The Duke of Sussex was the Prince Regent's fifth brother, Prince Augustus. He died unmarried in 1843, at the age of seventy.

12.   There was a distant family connection with the Wolfenbüttels. The Duke of Wolfenbüttel had been a cousin of George I, the great-great-grandfather of Princess Caroline.

13.   This absurd idea was still in vogue when Queen Victoria wanted Leopold's nephew, Prince Albert of Saxe-Coburg and Gotha, made a peer, but was ignored in 1947 on the marriage of the future Elizabeth II. In 1831, having previously declined the Greek throne, Prince Leopold was invited to become King of the Belgians. He married as his second wife Princess Louise of France, and became a highly valued confidant to Queen Victoria.

14.   Hibbert, *George IV: Regent*, p. 96.

15.   Hibbert, *George IV: Regent*, p. 98.

CHAPTER SIX

1.   Hibbert, *George IV: Regent*, p. 113.

2.   Christopher Hibbert (ed.), *Greville's England* (Folio Society, 1981), p. 68.

3.   Other members of the royal family who wed at this time included the Duke of Cumberland, later King of Hanover, who married Frederica of Mecklenburg, and the Duke of Cambridge, who married Augusta of Hesse-Cassel.

4.   In *George IV: Regent*, p. 129, Hibbert describes Victoria at the time of her christening as 'heir to the throne'. The heir was in fact her uncle, the Duke of York; then came the Duke of Clarence, and after him, her father. Thus in 1819 Princess Victoria was only fourth in line of succession. He states also, p. 115, that Victoria was the only child of the Duchess of Kent. By her previous marriage to Prince Charles of Leiningen-Dachsburg-Hardenburg the Duchess had given birth to a son, Prince Charles, Queen Victoria's half-brother, and to a daughter, Queen Victoria's half-sister and devoted companion, Princess Feodora.

5.   Royal Archives.

6.   Ibid.

7.   Ibid.

8.   Hibbert, *George IV: Regent*, p. 187.

Notes

9.   Hibbert, *George IV: Regent*, p. 193.

10.   Hibbert, *George IV: Regent*, p. 209.

11.   Hibbert, *George IV: Regent*, p. 223.

12.   George IV's Crimson Drawing Room was totally destroyed by fire in 1992, but has since been recreated.

13.   Sir Owen Morshead, *Windsor Castle* (Phaidon, 1951).

SELECT
BIBLIOGRAPHY

Place of publication is given only if outside London.

Brooke, John. *King George III*, Constable, 1972

Campbell, Cynthia. *The Most Polished Gentleman: George IV and the Women in his Life*, Kudos Books, 1995

Chevenix Trench, Charles. *The Royal Malady*, Longman, 1964

De-la-Noy, Michael. *The King Who Never Was: The Story of Frederick, Prince of Wales*, Peter Owen, 1996

———. *Windsor Castle: Past and Present*, Headline, 1990

Foord, Archibald S. *His Majesty's Opposition: 1714–1830*, Clarendon Press, 1964

Fraser, Flora. *The Unruly Queen: The Life of Queen Caroline*, Macmillan, 1996

Fulford, Roger. *Royal Dukes: The Father amd Uncles of Queen Victoria*, Duckworth, 1933

Grant Robertson, Charles. *England Under the Hanoverians*, Methuen, 1911.

Hedley, Olwen. *Queen Charlotte*, John Murray, 1975

Hibbert, Christopher. *George IV: Prince of Wales*, Longman, 1972

———. *George IV: Regent and King*, Allen Lane, 1975

Mansbridge, Michael. *John Nash: A Complete Catalogue*, Phaidon, 1991

Select Bibliography

Musgrave, Clifford. *Royal Pavilion: An Episode in the Romantic*, Leonard Hill, 1959

Plumb, J.H. *The First Four Georges*, B.T. Batsford, 1956

Prebble, John. *The King's Jaunt: George IV in Scotland, August 1822*, Collins, 1988

Richardson, Joanna. *The Disastrous Marriage: A Study of George IV and Caroline of Brunswick*, Jonathan Cape, 1960

———. *George IV: A Portrait*, Sidgwick & Jackson, 1966

Roberts, Henry. *A History of the Royal Pavilion, Brighton*, Country Life, 1939

Shane, Leslie. *The Life and Letters of Mrs Fitzherbert*, 2 vols, Burns & Oates, 1939–40

Smith, E.A. *A Queen on Trial: The Affair of Queen Caroline*, Stroud, Alan Sutton, 1993

Woodham-Smith, Cecil. *Queen Victoria: Her Life and Times, 1818–1861*, Hamish Hamilton, 1972

Ziegler, Philip. *King William IV*, Collins, 1971

POCKET BIOGRAPHIES

FORTHCOMING

W.G. Grace
Donald Trelford

The Brontës
Kathryn White

Lawrence of Arabia
Jeremy Wilson

Christopher Columbus
Peter Rivière

Martin Luther King
Harry Harmer

POCKET BIOGRAPHIES

AVAILABLE

David Livingstone
Christine Nicholls

Margot Fonteyn
Alastair Macaulay

Winston Churchill
Robert Blake

Abraham Lincoln
H.G. Pitt

Charles Dickens
Catherine Peters

Enid Blyton
George Greenfield

George IV
Michael De-la-Noy

Christopher Wren
James Chambers

Che Guevara
Andrew Sinclair

Beethoven
Anne Pimlott Baker

POCKET BIOGRAPHIES

For a copy of our complete list or details of other Sutton titles, please
contact Regina Schinner at Sutton Publishing Limited, Phoenix Mill,
Thrupp, Stroud, Gloucestershire, GL5 2BU